Electric
Locomotives

Brian Solomon

MBI

Dedication

To the memory of Alfred P. Solomon

On the front cover: Pennsylvania Railroad's GG1 electric was synonymous with speed, power, and progress. When the PRR electrified its New York–Washington, D.C., mainline in the 1930s, it was one of the most advanced railway lines in the world. On September 6, 1959, GG1 No. 4887 leads the *Afternoon Keystone* at Frankford Junction. *Richard Jay Solomon*

On the frontis: A freshly shopped and painted New Haven EF-4 leads a freight at Fresh Pond Junction in Queens, New York, in the autumn of 1964. Built by General Electric for the Virginian Railway, these electrics were sold to New Haven after Norfolk & Western bought the Virginian and discontinued its electric operations. The EF-4's layout followed contemporary diesel-electric practice and used a utilitarian road-switcher style. They were among the first rectifier electrics and used an Ignitron mercury-arc system to convert AC to DC for use by traction motors. *Richard Jay Solomon*

On the title page: In December 1981, shortly after they entered service, a pair of Amtrak AEM-7s leads a Boston-bound train at Pelham Bay Park in The Bronx. *Brian Solomon*

On the back cover, top: An Amtrak E60C races along the Northeast Corridor at Newark, Delaware, with a late-running train from Florida on the evening of December 22, 1992. *Brian Solomon* **Bottom:** New Haven made the unprecedented decision to electrify its lines with 11,000 volts at 25Hz. Despite a trend toward 25,000 volts at 60Hz for commercial transmission, former New Haven lines have retained the older standard in order to accommodate older equipment used in suburban services that cannot be easily converted.

Edited by Dennis Pernu
Designed by Kou Lor

Printed in China

CONTENTS

ACKNOWLEDGMENTS

Inherited my interest in railways and electric lo-comotives from my father, Richard Jay Solomon. His interest was in part inspired by my grandfather's gift to him of a Lionel train set that included a model of a Pennsylvania Railroad GG1. Although my grandfather had only a passing interest in trains, he always indulged us. The Lionel set gave my father years of enjoyment and inspiration in the 1940s and 1950s, and provided my brother, Seán, and I with entertainment a generation later. My family still owns the same set in working order—more than fifty years after they were bought new—which is a testimony to Lionel, but also a tribute to our fascination for the real trains they were modeled after.

My father began photographing railways in the 1950s, first shooting New York Central and New Haven electrics near his home in The Bronx, and then gradually traveling farther and farther from home until he ultimately circled the globe. Some of his first images were of the then-new New Haven EP5 electrics. As I write this, he is traveling with his venerable Leicas and a laptop to read my manuscript via e-mail. My father's photography inspired my own interest, which became my career and a lifelong project to document railway operations around the world. Both my father's photographs and my own provide many of the illustrations in this book. I also have included photos by Patrick Yough, Jim Shaughnessy, Robert A. Buck, Mel Patrick, John Gruber; from the collections of J. R. Quinn, and Tim Doherty; and by Otto Perry, via the Western History Collection at the Denver Public Library.

In researching this book I consulted dozens of sources. Without a doubt, some of my greatest inspirations are William D. Middleton's excellent books, especially his classic, *When the Steam Railroads Electrified*. Growing up I was enthralled with Karl Zimmerman's black-and-white pictorial, *The Remarkable GG1*. I'm on my second copy (the first fell apart after years of travel). I greatly enjoyed reading Al Staufer's books on Pennsy and New York Central locomotives. Other influential texts include P. Ransome-Wallis' *World Railway Locomotives,* and Ken Harris' *World Electric Locomotives*.

In addition, I obtained data and insight from a variety of railroad manuals, timetables, rulebooks, and brochures, and from articles in numerous magazines, including *TRAINS, The Railway Gazette, Today's Railways,* and *Railway Age.* Thanks, also, to the Irish Railway Record Society, Dublin, for the use of their extensive library.

Patrick Yough was greatly helpful in providing source information and tracking down technical details. John Gruber assisted with proofreading and supplied the sidebar on the North Shore *Electroliner.* Thanks to T. S. Hoover for accompanying me on numerous photographic trips and for proofreading. Markku Pulkkinen introduced me to the Swedish Dm3 electrics and supplied information on the Rc types. Every effort has been made to ensure accuracy, however, if errors appear, they are my own.

Special thanks to Dennis Pernu and everyone at MBI Publishing Company for making this project possible. Thanks, also, to my brother, who has spent many hours with me watching electric trains, and to my mother, Maureen Solomon, who has tolerated chatter about GG1s for several decades, and who accompanied the family on trips to watch GG1s in action many years ago.

INTRODUCTION

The Pennsylvania Railroad GG1 will always be my favorite electric. I'll never forget the thrill of a GG1 in action. The sounds of its motors accelerating, the clatter of its twenty wheels rolling through switch points or over a deck bridge, and the low rasping bark of its air horn are etched in my memory. The GG1 is at the root of my interest in electric railways. Before I was born, *TRAINS* magazine warned of the GG1's demise, yet the locomotives survived in revenue service long enough for me to experience them in person. My interest in watching, riding behind, and photographing them led to my research of why they were built, where they ran, how they worked, and why they were retired.

Writing about American electric locomotives has its challenges. American railways pioneered much of the technology used by electrified railways around the world, yet electric railways have always been something of an anomaly in the United States. Only a small percentage of the nation's lines have ever been electrified, and far fewer are electrified today than were fifty years ago. Nearly all of the interurban electric lines that once connected cities and towns across the country are gone. Many of the once-electrified heavy railroads gave up their wires for diesels. Economics ultimately favored electrification, but without the wires.

The diesel-electric locomotive is an electric locomotive that carries its powerplant on board, and electric railway technology made possible its development and perfection. While some cost-conscious American lines considered "straight electrics" as a quick way to eliminate expensive steam operations, nearly all ultimately opted for large-scale dieselization. The opposite was true in many other industrialized countries, where numerous lines were eventually electrified and diesel operations remain minimal, whether due to those nations' different economic systems, public ownership of transportation systems, energy

Perhaps the most famous of all GG1s was No. 4876, which made newspapers all over the country when it was involved in a disastrous wreck on January 15, 1953. Running out of control, it crashed through the bumper at Washington Union Station and landed in the concourse, which subsequently collapsed under the strain, sending the GG1 through the floor and into the basement. Spectacular as it was, not one person was killed, and No. 4876 was shipped back to Altoona for repair. Thirty years later it was still in daily service on NJ Transit. *Richard Jay Solomon*

costs and supplies, or ability to make long-term infrastructure commitments.

This book is intended to enlighten the reader on the development of heavy railway electrification in the United States, with a focus on the locomotives. The most significant are discussed in detail, including their dates of construction and operation, the traffic they were designed to haul, where they operated, and their performance statistics, such as starting tractive effort, maximum horsepower, and top operating speeds.

While the emphasis is on American machines, I've included a few photos of significant types in other countries. My hope is that you enjoy the photographs and feel that you have learned something about the railways and locomotives portrayed.

On the afternoon of June 30, 1959, New York Central T-2b No. 264 leads a train on the Harlem Division in The Bronx. New York Central's third-rail electrification was designed to eliminate the need for steam power into New York City as mandated by laws passed following a disastrous 1902 accident in the Park Avenue Tunnel. This locomotive was built by General Electric in 1917 and was slightly heavier than earlier B-B+B-B T-motors. *Richard Jay Solomon*

CHAPTER 1

STEAM-ERA ELECTRICS

The development of the steam locomotive in the first decades of the nineteenth century made possible the railway boom that began in Britain in the early 1820s, and which spread across the Atlantic within just a few years. Steam power was synonymous with the railway. Over the years, gradual refinement of locomotive design allowed for the operation of longer, heavier, and faster trains. Yet, the inherent limitations of steam locomotive design were long recognized by inventors and railway operators. Steam locomotives were dirty, inefficient, difficult to start, and costly to maintain and operate. From the 1830s onward, scientists and inventors experimented with electric motive power, often using battery-powered miniature locomotives. Harnessed electricity was a new form of power with great potential, but it was still undeveloped and impractical for large-scale experimentation, let alone daily railway operations.

In 1879, Werner von Siemens exhibited a small electric railway in Berlin. The event is often heralded as the first practical public demonstration of electric motive power using mechanically generated electricity. Inspired by Siemens and encouraged by Northern Pacific's Henry Villiard, Thomas A. Edison, the American electrical pioneer and founder of General Electric, began experimenting with electric railway propulsion in 1880. At the time, railway propulsion was considered the largest potential market for electricity.

Detail of Canadian National boxcab No. 6212. These steam-era machines worked Montreal suburban trains until 1995, when the line was re-electrified and new passenger multiple units entered service. *Brian Solomon*

America was among the first nations to apply electric traction for railway propulsion. Initial experiments were conducted on street railways and New York City's elevated lines. By the early 1890s, American engineers, including Leo Daft, Stephen Field, Frank J. Sprague, and others, were among the world leaders in electric railway technology. Sprague, a one-time employee of Edison, was responsible for many important innovations, including the first large-scale applications of electric propulsion on the Richmond Union Passenger Railway in Virginia in 1888. Sprague's success led to a booming business electrifying horse-drawn street railways and constructing new electric street railways. By the end of the 1890s the electrically powered trolley car had become a symbol of American progress,

The success of the electric street railway led to the development of electric interurban railways, lightweight lines that ran cross-country and connected cities and towns.

General Electric and Westinghouse Electric were the primary suppliers for electrical gear used on street and interurban cars and locomotives, as

Vintage Canadian National GE boxcab electrics pause with a suburban train at Val Royal Station in Montreal, Quebec, on the evening of January 11, 1993. The Canadian National predecessor Canadian Northern electrified its Mount Royal Tunnel and Montreal terminal during World War I using a 2,400-volt DC overhead system. The original locomotives built between 1914 and 1916 served this system for the better part of eighty years. Several are now preserved. *Brian Solomon*

well as the electrical infrastructure such as power stations and substations needed for electrical generation and distribution.

Because electric lines used cars that were smaller and lighter than those used by the well-established steam railways, their tracks and roadbeds were built to lighter standards. Nevertheless, in many cases the interurbans competed directly with the steam railways for passenger traffic and, in some cases, carried freight as well. Thus, electrics represented a serious threat to the established railroads, which had enjoyed near monopolies on transportation. Railroads responded in various ways. Some, such as the New Haven and Southern Pacific, acquired interurban lines and operated them in parallel with their steam railroad services. Although steam railroads viewed these electric newcomers as unwelcome competition, it did not take long before they looked to harness electric traction themselves.

Pros and Cons of Electrification

Although heavy railway electrification was the outgrowth of electric street railways and interurbans, railroads were slow to explore its full potential. The earliest electric propulsion systems were not powerful enough to propel heavy mainline trains. In the mid-1890s both the New Haven and Pennsylvania Railroads experimented with short sections electrified with technology more akin to the light trolley lines of the period than the electrification that steam railroads subsequently developed.

The prospect of major steam railway electrification was controversial during the last decade

Although the last American side-rod electrics were retired more than 30 years ago, they survive in Sweden as of this writing. Class Dm3 three-section side-rod electrics are used in the Arctic to move heavy iron ore trains from mines near Kiruna and Gällivare to ports at Narvik in Norway, and Luleå on the Gulf of Bothnia in Sweden. The big side-rod electrics have proven well suited to difficult Arctic conditions. In July 2002, a Dm3 leads a train at Torne Träsk, Sweden, a location far north of the Arctic Circle. *Brian Solomon*

A Swedish Dm3 waits on a passing siding at Harrtträskvägen with an empty ore train. These locomotives draw power from overhead lines energized at 15kV at 16.6Hz. Transformers feed single-phase commutator motors (two per section for a total of six motors per locomotive) that produce a starting tractive effort of 176,000 pounds. The Dm3 was introduced in 1960 and built as late as 1970. *Brian Solomon*

of the nineteenth century and first decades of the twentieth century. Proponents of electrification claimed numerous potential advantages. Electrification was a more efficient use of energy and could lower fuel, labor, and maintenance costs. Electric motors provided greater starting power than steam power, and could simplify operations through the use of double-ended equipment and the elimination of fuel and water stops. However, the most conspicuous advantages of electrification from the public viewpoint were significantly cleaner, quieter, and possibly faster trains. These latter considerations, as much as the potential of gaining operational efficiency, encouraged the installation of America's first heavy-duty electrification.

Despite the many prospective advantages of electrification, there were drawbacks. In the early years, there was a lack of interest by steam railroads for serious investment. Despite the allure of potentially lower operating costs, high initial capital costs made it difficult for railroads to justify investment. In addition to the great expense of electrical supply equipment and specialized locomotives, electrification required separate shops and specialized mechanics. More sophisticated and expensive signaling equipment was also needed in electrified zones to prevent electrical transmissions from interfering with signal track circuits. Then there were safety concerns regarding the hazards posed by high-voltage lines; this danger fueled the opponents of electrification, who used scare tactics to enrage the public.

Early Electrics
In 1893, General Electric built its first commercial electric locomotive for steam railway service at its Lynn, Massachusetts, facility. In his book, *When the Steam Railroads Electrified*, William D. Middleton describes it as a 30-ton, four-wheel machine, capable of 30 miles per hour. GE built a second, larger locomotive in 1894 that used a pair of trucks and nose-suspended traction motors. (A nose-suspended motor is supported on one end by the axle and on other end by the truck frame. It typically uses single-reduction gearing to power the axle.)

This original steeple cab had a long career working a cotton mill in Taftville, Connecticut. It was retired in 1964, and today is displayed at the Connecticut Trolley Museum at Warehouse Point, Connecticut. Steeple-cab electrics of a similar design became a standard type for electric railways.

In the 1890s, the Baltimore & Ohio simplified its Baltimore terminal area operations by building a new Belt Line through the city that included a

long tunnel beneath a residential downtown area. To overcome public opposition to locomotive smoke soiling residential areas, the railroad made the unprecedented decision to electrify its new line.

Electric operations were inaugurated in June 1895. General Electric supplied electrical equipment and locomotives for B&O's three-mile Baltimore Belt Line electrification, which included a 1.25-mile tunnel. The system was derived from 600-volt direct current systems employed by most contemporary street railways. Initially, B&O employed three steeple-cab locomotives built by GE. Propulsion was provided by four gearless, 360-horsepower, direct current electric motors. Motor armatures engaged hollow quills surrounding the driving axles and powered, spoked driving wheels that used rubber blocks to provide a flexible connection that cushioned shocks to the motors.

Initially, B&O used a rigid, fixed overhead system to supply electricity to the locomotives. In 1900, a more conventional over-running third rail, similar to that used on the recently electrified New York City elevated rapid transit lines, replaced the original system. Baltimore & Ohio's pioneering electrification was America's only significant mainline electric operation for the better part of a decade and set important precedents for later electric operations.

Baltimore & Ohio bought additional electric locomotives from General Electric between 1909 and 1912, and between 1923 and 1927. The advent of modern diesel-electrics negated the need for the Belt Line electrification, and Baltimore & Ohio discontinued electric operations in the early 1950s.

Grand Central Electrification
By the end of the nineteenth century, New York City was the largest city in the United States, and its burgeoning population had resulted in one of the first significant suburban railway networks that allowed workers to live much farther from the city than had been practical in earlier times. New York Central's Park Avenue Tunnel to Grand

Central Depot was the only passenger route to Manhattan that didn't require a ferry ride. Grand Central was shared with the New York, New Haven & Hartford, which reached it by way of trackage rights over New York Central's Harlem Division from Woodlawn Junction in The Bronx. By the 1890s, the two railroads were operating roughly 500 daily trains through the tunnel, making Grand Central one of the busiest terminals in the world.

Although it was enlarged in 1898, Grand Central was clearly inadequate for the traffic volume. Space constraints made expansion difficult, so New York Central was keen on the construction of an entirely new terminal, but stifled by the high cost of Manhattan real estate. According to William D. Middleton in his book, *Grand Central: The World's Greatest Railway Terminal,* in 1899, William J. Wilgus, a New York Central vice president and chief engineer, envisioned a novel two-level, underground terminal that maximized space by allowing air rights to be leased on the buildings above it. Such a terminal, however, could not be operated using conventional steam power because smoke emissions would make it impossible to see or breathe in the tunnels. Electrification was the obvious solution. Sadly, while New York Central was pondering electrification, disaster struck forcing the issue.

On the morning of January 8, 1902, an inbound New York Central passenger train approaching Grand Central overran a smoke-obscured stop signal in the Park Avenue Tunnel demolishing a standing New Haven suburban train. Fifteen people were killed and many seriously injured. The media sensationalized the accident, fueling public outrage. Sentiment was already polarized against the large railroads, which were perceived as monopolists preying on a hapless public. Despite their political power, the tide was beginning to turn against the railroads' heavy-handed business practices. New York State swiftly enacted legislation that banned steam locomotive operation in Manhattan and precipitated one of most significant motive power developments in railroad history.

To comply with the new laws, New York City's railroads were forced to pioneer practical electric railroad technology.

New York Central established the Electric Traction Commission (ETC), a think tank of the nation's foremost experts on electrical engineering, including Wilgus, Sprague, and George Gibbs. Studying the applications of electric railway traction on street railways, Baltimore & Ohio's Belt Line electrification, and recent third-rail electrification on elevated rapid transit lines in Manhattan and Brooklyn, the ETC concluded that a 660-volt, direct current system delivered by outside third-rail best suited their application.

New York Central's First Electric

Working with New York Central's ETC in 1904, GE designed and built No. 6000, a double-ended locomotive with a 1-D-1 wheel arrangement. (In electric locomotive terminology, letters describe powered axles, numbers unpowered axles. "A" indicates one powered axle, "B" two powered axles, "C" three powered axles, and "D" four powered axles, while "1" denotes one unpowered axle, and so on. This is contrary to steam locomotive practice, which uses numbers to indicate wheels and groups them in pre-established configurations to define which are powered and unpowered.)

NYC 6000 featured a typical center-cab configuration powered by four 550-horsepower bipolar (two pole) traction motors that produced 2,200 horsepower of combined continuous output. Short-term output of up to 3,000 horsepower was possible for starting and rapid acceleration. Like the early B&O electrics, 6000 used a gearless traction-motor design, but in this case motor poles were mounted on the locomotive frame, and armatures directly on the axles. The poles and armatures were spring-loaded to maintain flexibility. According to Brian Hollingsworth in *The Illustrated Encyclopedia of North American Locomotives,* the total locomotive weight was 200,500 pounds, with approximately 142,000 pounds on driving wheels, giving the machine a maximum axle load of about 35,500 pounds. The locomotive

Working in anonymity as New York Central No. 100, the railroad's first electric drills Mott Haven Yard at 140th Street in The Bronx on November 28, 1958. More than fifty years earlier, this machine was featured in newspapers and magazines around the world when it demonstrated the capabilities of heavy electric traction and tested at speeds in excess of 80 miles per hour. *Richard Jay Solomon*

was designed to haul a standard 450-ton passenger train, but was capable of hauling trains weighing almost twice that amount.

Largely the work of GE's Asa Batchlelder, 6000 also incorporated important innovations from Sprague, including the first documented application of his electro-pneumatic multiple-unit (MU) control system on a locomotive. Sprague's MU control was developed in 1897 to allow two or more electric units (railcars or, in this case, locomotives) to be operated synchronously under the control of a single engineer (operator). Today nearly all diesel-electric locomotives are built with MU controls and it is standard practice

to operate locomotives in multiple. The ability to operate electric locomotives (and subsequently diesel-electric locomotives) in multiple was one of the great advantages of electric motive power over steam, dramatically increasing the amount of work one person could do.

Initially listed as Class L, 6000 was soon reclassified as T. Later, following modifications discussed below, the class was changed a second time to S-motor. In its later years, locomotive 6000 was renumbered 100 and was the railroad's sole S-1 electric. In 1905, it was used in extensive experiments on a six-mile electrified test track parallel to New York Central's Water Level Route mainline in the shadow of GE's plant at Schenectady, New York. Satisfied with the capabilities of the prototype, New York Central ordered a fleet of 34 similar locomotives from GE for its express and long-distance passenger service to Grand Central. These were originally classed as T-2, but were soon reclassified as S-2. New York Central's suburban services were handled by electric multiple-units (self-propelled passenger cars) instead of by locomotive-hauled trains.

Although New York Central was undertaking ambitious plans for an all-new Grand Central Terminal, it first had to comply with the ban on steam power that went into effect July 1, 1908. The old Grand Central was electrified as an interim operation while the new terminal was built around it. The first electric services began on September 20, 1906; by 1907, the station was mostly electrified. Initially, electric services only extended a few miles beyond Manhattan, but Central gradually extended the electrification to take better advantage of electric power and minimize the need for engine changes. By the mid-1920s, the third rail extended 33 miles north of Grand Central to Croton-on-Hudson (now known as Croton-Harmon) on its famous Hudson Division,

to North White Plains on its Harlem Division, and on the Getty Square Branch of its former Putnam Division. In the 1920s and early 1930s, Central electrified its West Side freight line in Manhattan.

Within days of the initiation of electric service, Central endured another disastrous accident when a locomotive-hauled train derailed at speed, killing 23 people. Ironically, this accident demonstrated the fallibility of the new electric service that had been introduced in specific response to the earlier crash. The second disaster, like the first, had serious repercussions. Wilgus resigned, and New York Central was forced to reevaluate the design of its electric locomotives. Sensational press reports propelled technical details of railway operation into public consciousness and resulted in a greater demand for safety. New York Central took action by rebuilding all of its electrics with leading bogie-trucks in place of pony trucks, resulting in a 2-D-2 wheel arrangement. Central classed them as S-motors to reflect this change.

In 1908 and 1909, New York Central ordered 12 additional electrics from General Electric, and classed them as S-3. Several, including the pioneer, have been preserved, though none have been restored for public display.

New York Central's Later Electrics

Between 1913 and 1926, General Electric built more advanced electric locomotives for New York Central. These were also classified as T-motors, but they should not be confused with the original "T" description. Central listed 36 Class T's in five of subclasses that reflected slight variations on the design. These T-motors used an end-cab design with an articulated B-B+B-B wheel arrangement in which all wheels were powered. This allowed for a significantly more powerful locomotive with the full weight of the machine placed on the

In August 1961, New York Central's pioneering S-motor was still hard at work, switching at the railroad's Mott Haven Yard in The Bronx. Built in 1904 and originally numbered 6000, in later years the sole S-1 carried the number 100. This machine was preserved for posterity, but as of this writing is not available for public display. *Richard Jay Solomon*

Just after sunset in July 1963, a New York Central T-motor leads a Grand Central–bound passenger train past a suburban station along the Hudson River. *Richard Jay Solomon*

At 3 P.M. on February 8, 1959, New York Central T-3a No. 280 leads a six-car suburban train at Woodlawn Junction in The Bronx, the point where the New Haven's line from Boston joined the New York Central's Harlem Division for the run into Grand Central. *Richard Jay Solomon*

driving wheels, yet with a lighter axle load since the weight was distributed more equally.

Because the T-motors used an articulated arrangement, and smaller, lighter traction motors, they were much less damaging to tracks than S-motors. As a result, they held the majority of road passenger assignments, with the S-motors largely relegated to switching services. The T-motors worked Central's passenger trains until the Penn-Central era, when former New Haven dual-mode (diesel-electric/electric) EMD-built FL9s (see Chapter 2) were assigned to former New York Central services, allowing for the elimination of the Croton-Harmon and North White Plains engine changes.

In the 1920s, New York Central ordered seven Class Q motors from GE that used steeple-cab design with a B-B wheel arrangement. Another type of B-B locomotive was the end-cab Class R. Central also ordered a fleet of R-1 electrics for its Detroit River Tunnel electrification, which, like the New York electrification, used direct current under-running third rail.

Precedent-Setting New York Central Electrics

Significant to the development of later diesel-electrics were two classes of GE electrics. These were big machines, one class with a 2-C+C-2 wheel arrangement built in 1928 for Central's Cleveland Union Terminal (CUT) electrification, and 42 R-2s that were built in 1930 for Central's West Side freight operations in Manhattan and used a C-C arrangement with six-motors, one driving each axle. Both types used state-of-art, nose-suspended traction motors with single-reduction gearing to power the driving axles, an arrangement similar to that used by electric trolley cars since the 1890s.

Traditional electric motors suffered from a low power-to-weight ratio, and a nose-suspended motor sufficiently powerful for heavy locomotive applications would have placed excessive weight on axles, making them impractical. Advances in motor technology in the 1920s, however, allowed the development of powerful nose-suspended motors that were light enough for heavy-locomotive

On the evening of May 23, 1968, a pair of South Shore 700 series electrics, former New York Central class R-2s, moves freight at Burnham Yard in suburban Chicago. In total, South Shore rebuilt seven R-2s, numbering them 701 to 707. The first was completed in 1955, the last 12 years later. Each of these locomotives used six GE 286B traction motors, one to power each axle. *John Gruber*

application. This development made obsolete most of the early methods of DC motor-transmission, such as the quill drives.

While the new nose-suspended motors were easily applied to moderate-speed DC electrics, it would be another two decades before this technology was standard on all electric locomotive designs. The nose-suspended motor combined with lightweight high-output diesel engines developed by the U. S. Navy for submarine use first made possible the development of practical high-output diesel-electric locomotives in the 1930s. Later, the perfection of nose-suspended DC traction motors and improved truck designs for mass-produced diesel-electrics paved the way for their eventual use on high-voltage straight electrics (see Chapter 2). Today, powerful and compact nose-suspended motors with single-reduction gearing are standard on most of the world's diesel-electric and straight-electric locomotives.

Of special interest to modern locomotive design were Central's R-2 electrics, not just because of their nose-suspended motors, but because they employed a C-C wheel arrangement (a pair of three-axle/three-motor trucks). This same arrangement has subsequently become the predominant arrangement on most American road diesels today. Yet, Central's pioneering use of C-C arrangement predated its standard use on American lines by nearly three decades.

In actual service, Central's R-2 electrics were relatively obscure and primarily used on freight services on the West Side route, and thus often relegated to nocturnal operation. In later years, a few R-2s were assigned to Central's Detroit River Tunnel electrified line. Between 1955 and 1958 seven former R-2s were rebuilt for freight services on Chicago-area interurban Chicago, South Shore & South Bend's 1,500-volt DC overhead lines. Numbered 701 to 707, they were painted in South Shore's attractive orange livery. According to *South Shore . . . The Last Interurban* by William D. Middleton, these R-2s were equipped with pantographs and other electric equipment from the Cleveland Union Terminal electrics, which were rebuilt for New York Central's third-rail lines about the same time (see below). Middleton notes that, in rebuilt form, the 700 series locomotives each weighed 280,000 pounds and delivered 66,000 pounds starting tractive effort (based on 25 percent adhesion). South Shore rated the 700s at 3,000 horsepower and allowed them 60 miles per hour maximum speed. Some of these locomotives worked South Shore freight services until the early 1970s.

The Cleveland Union Terminal (CUT) electrics were originally designated "P-1a." After the CUT overhead electrification was discontinued in favor

June 30, 1959 was pleasant and sunny as New York Central P-2b led a passenger train at Williamsbridge in The Bronx. This view clearly shows New York Central's under-running third rail. Electrical contact was made from below, rather than above, as with over-running third rail.
Richard Jay Solomon

New York Central P-2b leads a long-distance passenger train past Spuyten Duyvil station in New York City. P-motors were substantially larger than T-motors and are easily identified by the large front "porch" ahead of the cab. Like most American electrics, the P-motors had cabs at both ends. *Richard Jay Solomon*

of dieselization in the 1950s, the P-motors were rebuilt (receiving new subclasses, P-2a and P-2b) for third-rail operation on the Grand Central electrified lines. These big electrics worked for the next 15 years hauling Central's legendary Great Steel Fleet between Grand Central and Croton-Harmon, and suburban trains to North White Plains.

AC versus DC Systems
In the first decades of commercial electric enterprise there erupted a raging controversy regarding

New York Central operated an unusual fleet of tri-power locomotives on its electrified New York City lines. Developed by GE and Alco, they could operate as straight third-rail electrics, as battery-electrics from onboard storage cells, or as battery-electric/diesel-electrics drawing power from both the batteries and the onboard diesel engine. They were designed for switching services, where they needed to work beyond the limits of the third rail and in confined areas where fumes from an internal combustion engine were prohibited. New York Central No. 539 is seen drawing current from the third rail at Harmon, New York, in May 1955. *J. R. Quinn collection*

Appalachian coal hauler Virginian electrified in the mid-1920s using an 11,000-volt AC overhead system. Initially, it used extremely powerful boxcab electrics built by Alco and Westinghouse in 1925. Designated EL-3A, these machines used phase converters to turn single-phase current to three-phase for use by large asynchronous AC induction motors. The motors engaged driving wheels with a jackshaft and side-rod connection as pictured here. Although the three-phase AC motors delivered enormous power, they were limited to just two running speeds. *Richard Jay Solomon*

direct current versus alternating current systems. The controversy polarized the principle electrical suppliers: General Electric promoted DC systems, Westinghouse promoted AC. While AC was more efficient for distribution on large-scale power grids, DC was better understood at the time of the first heavy railway electrification, and thus preferred. Nearly all electrified street railways and interurbans used direct current and the operation of DC motors was well established.

As AC technology matured, the debate continued. DC transmission systems were simpler than AC and were more efficient and easier to control for railway applications. However, DC requires frequent, expensive substations to maintain adequate power levels, and the development of practical transformers in the 1880s made AC a better choice for large-scale, long-distance electrification schemes. By using transformers, AC can be more efficiently transmitted over long distances, with the voltage stepped up or down as required for distribution and consumption. On the downside, AC generation and transmission is significantly more complex, since AC motors are larger and require more sophisticated control equipment. AC induction motors are

Three-unit Virginian side-rod electric No. 103 departs Roanoke, Virginia, with a 107 westbound extra hopper train on August 7, 1932. These machines, built by Alco with Westinghouse electric gear in summer 1925, were semi-permanently coupled and considered by the railroad as one EL-3A locomotive. Each of the three sections was powered by a pair of three-phase induction motors. The combined weight was more than 1.2 million pounds, and the combined starting tractive effort was a phenomenal 231,000 pounds. *Otto Perry, Western History Collection, Denver Public Library, OP19654*

more powerful and comparatively simple compared to DC motors, operate at constant speed and constant torque. The three-phase distribution required necessitates dual catenary, a much more difficult operational design.

The lack of suitable single-phase AC motor for railway traction initially made high-voltage, single-phase AC impractical for railways. According to "A History of the Development of the Single-Phase System," published by Westinghouse in the 1890s, Westinghouse engineer Benjamin G. Lamme developed a single-phase series-commutator motor operationally similar to DC motors and featuring variable speed control ideal for railway traction. It was a triumph for Westinghouse's AC systems and

gave credence to their arguments in favor of AC traction. The publication elaborated, "From the speed control standpoint, the single-phase system was far ahead of the direct-current, for the flexibility of the alternating-current system allowed voltage variations for controlling motor speed without the use of regulating rheostats for absorbing the extra voltage and power [necessary with DC systems]."

Westinghouse teamed up with Baldwin to build electric locomotives; Baldwin manufactured mechanical components and Westinghouse supplied electrical gear. A few years later, GE teamed up with Alco in the construction of electric locomotives. Conveniently, GE and Alco both had primary manufacturing facilities at Schenectady,

New York. Later, GE and Alco became closely involved in the manufacture of diesels, while Baldwin and Westinghouse were similarly linked.

In 1896, GE and Westinghouse agreed on a patent pool allowing both manufacturers to sell either DC or AC technology. Despite the exchange, GE continued to promote DC, while Westinghouse went on to pioneer early high-voltage AC railway traction.

By the early twentieth century, these developments provided three primary types of electrical systems for railway traction: direct current, single-phase AC, and three-phase AC. Yet, there were few established standards even among common types of electrification. The basic electrification configurations for supplying current were low-voltage DC (550 to 750 volts) transmitted with either third rail (such as New York Central's under-running variety) or overhead trolley wire (as used by street railways); moderate-voltage DC (between 1,200 and 3,000 volts) with overhead wire; high-voltage, single-phase AC (typically 11,000 volts at 25Hz in the U.S.); and three-phase AC. Most of the electrification in North America was either DC or single-phase AC. The only major American application of three-phase AC supply was Great Northern's original Cascade electrification, discussed later in the chapter.

New Haven Pioneers Single Phase AC

As New York Central was undertaking its third-rail DC electrification of Grand Central, the New

New Haven EP-1 electric No. 032 leads an eight-car passenger train eastward on the railroad's four-track electrified mainline between Stamford and New Haven, Connecticut, on October 16, 1930. New Haven's EP-1s were numbered 01 to 041. Each had four traction motors and a one-hour rating of 817 horsepower. Heavy trains routinely required two units. The EP-1s were capable of 88 miles per hour. *Otto Perry, Western History Collection, Denver Public Library, OP 13744*

Three of New Haven's original EF-1 freight electrics lead a westward freight at approximately 45 miles per hour near Stratford, Connecticut, on October 16, 1930. The EF-1s, numbered 076 to 111, were built by Baldwin-Westinghouse and used a geared-quill drive. Each had a one-hour rating of 1,120 horsepower and was routinely used in multiple to haul heavy tonnage. Three EF-1s had roughly the same pulling power as a single EF-4 rectifier. *Otto Perry, Western History Collection, Denver Public Library, OP 13745*

Haven Railroad was faced with difficult decisions. It operated over New York Central trackage to reach Grand Central and needed to embrace electric operations. Like New York Central, it faced time constraints in developing practical electric motive power. Yet New Haven faced a serious quandary regarding electrification. As mentioned earlier, it carried an exceptional volume of suburban passenger traffic to New York City.

One option, and perhaps the easiest short-term solution, was a locomotive swap near Woodlawn in The Bronx, the junction with New York Central's Harlem Division. Despite the obvious logic of this choice, New Haven decided it was impractical because of the high costs of building an engine terminal at Woodlawn and the delays to suburban service that an engine change would incur. Also, New Haven hoped to take long-term advantage of electrified operations and a Woodlawn engine change would be no more than a temporary solution.

New Haven was well versed with DC electrification; it had been experimenting with both overhead and third-rail trolley-like systems since the

New Haven EF-1 boxcabs 088 and 085 are seen at the railroad's namesake on August 18, 1937. The 36 EF-1s were built during 1912 and 1913 and were strictly designed for freight service. They were not equipped for DC operation and did not have third-rail shoes. *Otto Perry, Western History Collection, Denver Public Library, OP 13720*

1890s. Based on this experience, and on New York Central's choice of DC third rail for the Grand Central electrification, it would have been easy enough for New Haven to adopt this standard for its lines. In "Twenty Years of Electrical Operations on the New York, New Haven & Hartford," written in the 1920s, W. L. Bean, one of the New Haven's principal electrical engineers, explained that the railroad carefully considered four systems of electrification: 600-volt DC with third-rail delivery, similar to that which New York Central selected and nearly identical to New Haven's experimental branch-line electrification; 1,200-volt DC with overhead transmission, a popular system on interurban electric lines; 11,000-volt, 15-cycle, single-phase AC; and

11,000-volt, 25-cycle, single-phase AC. The latter two systems were basically untried, with no precedent for heavy mainline electrification. Bean explained that the 11,000-volt, 25-cycle, single-phase AC system was chosen "because it provided economical transmission of power and imposed no limit to the extension of the electrification." He went on to state, "Later experience has confirmed the wisdom of this course and demonstrated, in addition, the high flexibility of this system. The 25-cycle system has the advantage over the 15-cycle system in that power can be more readily purchased if desired."

New Haven's bold decision to electrify with high-voltage AC was taken because the railroad had visions of eventually electrifying most of its mainline operations, not just the New York terminal district, and AC was more practicable for a large-scale project.

Initially the railroad electrified from Woodlawn Junction, New York, to Stamford, Connecticut, opening that stretch for regular service in July 1907. By 1915, wires had reached New Haven. The railroad's electrification reached its zenith in 1927 when it energized the Harlem River Line and the New York Connecting Railroad over Hell Gate Bridge and completed electrification of New York City–area freight terminal trackage. In addition to its New Haven-to-New York mainlines, New Haven's branches to both New Canaan and Danbury, Connecticut, were also electrified with high-voltage AC, as was its New York, Westchester & Boston affiliate. The NYW&B was a newly built line that operated, in part, parallel to New Haven's own tracks and was specifically designed to handle suburban passenger traffic, removing some congestion from the Grand Central route. In total, New Haven had 672 track miles under wire by the end of the 1920s.

At first New Haven provided all of its own electricity, generating power at its Cos Cob, Connecticut, plant using four steam turbines. After 1915, New Haven augmented Cos Cob with commercially generated power.

New Haven's AC electrification was the first of its type worldwide and represented a technological leap over DC systems. In addition to electrifying its New York suburban passenger operations, it also accommodated its high-speed, long-distance passenger traffic, and eventually freight traffic moving in and out of New York City. Although the railroad's AC catenary never made it any further east than its sprawling Cedar Hill Yard, near its Connecticut namesake, the New Haven Railroad had intentions of eventually extending electric operations to Boston and from New Haven to Springfield, Massachusetts. (New Haven's electric ambitions had even predated New York City's mandate; the railroad had left provisions for overhead wire in the construction of Boston's South Station in the late 1890s.) Unfortunately, its finances collapsed in the wake of its early electrification schemes. Wires eventually reached Boston under Amtrak, more than 30 years after New Haven's forced inclusion in Penn-Central. A mural inside the Hartford, Connecticut, railroad station portrays high-voltage electric operations there, a lasting indication of New Haven's original ambitions.

When New Haven announced that it had chosen a radical and untried high-voltage AC system, it fueled the debate over railway electrification. Some authorities claimed high-voltage AC was an unworkable choice, and many steam railway men and members of the public were distrustful of New Haven's new electric services. New Haven was on a tight schedule to electrify its operations, and when electric services began in 1907, a few bugs in the system resulted in well-publicized service failures. The January 15, 1909, issue of *The Railway Gazette,* published in Britain, reported "the suburban travellers have been loud in their complaints regarding defective service."

As with many new operations, early failures led critics to denounce the virtues of the whole system as well as the technology. New Haven had introduced the most extensive mainline electrification in the world and every detail of its operation was subject to scrutiny. In order to silence critics and set the record straight, on December 11, 1908, W. S. Murray, an electrical engineer for New Haven, delivered a detailed report to the American Institute of Electrical Engineers. Reprinted in the same issue of *The Railway Gazette* previously cited, Murray noted, "Unlike steam traction, where the number of links in the delay chain is but one, electric traction has its delay chain composed of three links; namely the power house, line and locomotives. The failure in anyone of these links may produce train delay or delays."

It appears that the majority of New Haven's early service failures were attributable to disruptions with its Cos Cob power station and problems with the design of the overhead catenary that delivered power to the trains.

All of this might just be an obscure footnote in railway history if New Haven's electrification had been unsuccessful. Quite contrary, not only was the electrification a success for the railroad, it also established trends in the development of electrified railways throughout the United States and around the world. Today, high-voltage AC electrification is the preferred system on many lines worldwide.

New Haven's Early Electric Locomotives

New Haven turned to Westinghouse, the chief proponent of AC systems, to supply its electrification system, locomotives, and passenger multiple-units. Baldwin-Westinghouse built its first batch of 41 locomotives between 1906 and 1908. Originally they were four-axle (B-B) machines riding on pairs of swiveling trucks and suffered from a lateral hunting, a tracking problem also known as "nosing." As a result they were fitted with unpowered pony trucks within their first couple of years of operation. These machines, numbered 01 through 041 were designed for passenger service and in later years classified as EP-1s ("EP" denoting "electric passenger"). They were 37 feet, 7.5 inches long, and after the pony trucks were fitted weighed 217,600 pounds each. Westinghouse Type 130 gearless motors rated at 350 horsepower

New Haven 114 was an EF-2 motor-generator locomotive built by General Electric and Alco. Rated at 1,350 horsepower and designed for a maximum speed of 42 miles per hour, the EF-2 was faster and more powerful than the older EF-1 type. This locomotive had been withdrawn from active service when it was photographed at Van Nest Shops in March 1958.
Richard Jay Solomon

A pair of New Haven's EP-2 electrics sits outside the railroad's Van Nest Shops in The Bronx on March 8, 1958. The locomotive on the left wears New Haven's traditional livery, the machine on the right is in the 1950s-era McGinnis scheme. *Richard Jay Solomon*

each were used for power. The motor armatures drove hollow quills that surrounded the drive-wheel axles. Power was transmitted to the wheels using discs that engaged the wheels with spring connections. This type of flexible drive connection minimized physical shocks to the traction motors without the necessity of gearing. Since the

locomotives needed to work in both New York Central and New Haven electrified districts, traction motors were designed to operate from both single-phase AC and DC power.

The EP-1s were designed to operate either singly or in multiple, and although New York Central's S-motors shared this design characteristic, in

A detailed view of the retractable third-rail shoe on a New Haven EP-3 boxcab electric. This shoe was designed to draw DC power from either an over-running or under-running third rail. *Richard Jay Solomon*

On June 22, 1958, a New Haven EF-3 electric leads a short freight across the Hell Gate Bridge. The New York Connecting Railroad's Hell Gate Bridge Route provided New Haven with access to New York's Pennsylvania Station and allowed for through passenger services between Boston and Washington, D.C. Today it is a vital link for Amtrak's Northeast Corridor. *Richard Jay Solomon*

A view inside New Haven Railroad's Van Nest Shops reveals the wheels and motors of an EP-2 electric alongside EP-4 No. 364. Notice the dual-traction motors used to power the center axle and the gear on the quill of outside axle. Each of an EP-2's six powered axles would have been powered by such a dual set of traction motors that engaged a geared hollow quill surrounding the running axle. The quill engaged the wheel using a flexible spring-cup system with cups located between the spokes. *Richard Jay Solomon*

practice New Haven was the first railroad to make regular use of electric locomotives working in multiple. The EP-1s were designed to singly haul 200 tons and, according to Westinghouse, maintain an average speed of 26 miles per hour between stations 2.2 miles apart. In actual service, they were capable of moving up to 390 tons. In the early years of New Haven electric operation, 73 to 75 percent of passenger trains could be pulled with a single EP-1 locomotive. The remaining trains were operated with pairs of electrics. Ironically, al-though New Haven had intended to use the electrics in this building-block principle of loco-motive assignment, observers of the railway, ig-norant to the design intentions, misconstrued the doubling of locomotives on heavy trains as a design failure.

During 1910 and 1911, New Haven took de-livery of several experimental locomotives that variously employed geared and side-rod drives. Then, during 1912 and 1913, Baldwin-Westinghouse built a fleet of 36 freight locomotives, Class EF-1.

These featured a 1-B-B-1 wheel arrangement, following the precedent established by the early types, but used a geared-quill drive instead of a gearless quill. Since these locomotives did not need to operate to Grand Central, they were only designed for work from the AC overhead catenary. They weighed 219,500 pounds each, with 165,000 pounds on driving wheels. Using Westinghouse 409C AC traction motors with a 17:97 gear ratio, the EF-1 delivered 21,200 pounds tractive effort with a one-hour rating, and 14,760 pounds continuously.

In addition to road locomotives, New Haven also ordered a small fleet of electrics for switching service in its freight yards. These were substantially lighter than the electrics for road service. From the beginning of electric operations, New Haven also operated a fleet of electric passenger multiple units (self-propelled passenger cars) in suburban service.

Between 1919 and 1927, Baldwin-Westinghouse built 27 large passenger electrics, classed EP-2. Although these used an unusual 1-C-1+1-C-1 wheel arrangement, they were technologically similar to the EF-1 and EP-1 electrics that dominated New Haven's road fleet. According to Westinghouse data, they were powered by Westinghouse 409-C2 AC traction motors using geared-quill drives like those employed in the EF-1s. The initial batch of five EP-2s delivered in 1919, weighed 350,000 pounds each, with 233,000 pounds on driving wheels and a 27:87 gear ratio delivered 47,520 pounds maximum tractive effort, 18,000 pounds tractive effort with a one-hour rating and 12,540 pounds continuously. Their continuous output was a little more than 2,000 horsepower, double that of the EP-1s. In express passenger service they were rated to haul 900 tons.

While most of New Haven's early electric locomotives were Baldwin-Westinghouse products, General Electric also built several experimental electrics, including five road locomotives and two switchers in 1926 using a motor-generator arrangement that permitted the use of DC traction motors.

While these machines remained relatively obscure on New Haven, GE perfected motor-generator technology and later sold motor-generator electrics to other lines. These are discussed in greater detail later in the text. In later years, GE superceded Baldwin-Westinghouse as New Haven's primary electric locomotive supplier.

In the 1930s and early 1940s, General Electric built several classes of electrics for the New Haven, including ten EP-3 articulated boxcabs in 1931. Designed for 70-mile-per-hour passenger service, they used the 2-C+C-2 wheel arrangement developed a few years earlier for the Cleveland Union Terminal electrics. New Haven's EP-3s were 77 feet long with a 66-foot wheelbase. They used six twin-arm, 12-pole motors (one for each powered axle) with quill-and-cup drives providing a continuous 2,740 horsepower and a 3,440-horsepower one-hour rating (in AC territory). When operating in DC third-rail territory to reach Grand Central, motor output was slightly lower. The type delivered 68,400 pounds starting tractive effort. The EP-3's high output and excellent tracking qualities at higher speeds convinced Pennsylvania Railroad to borrow one for testing in 1934 when it was designing its new electric motor for its Northeast Corridor operations.

In 1938, New Haven placed a repeat order with GE for six EP-4 electrics. Based on the EP-3 design, the EP-4s were similar to the EP-3s in most respects but featured a handsome double-ended streamlined carbody and were somewhat more powerful. They provided 3,600-horsepower continuous output, and were designed to operate up to 93 miles per hour. In 1943, Alco-GE and Baldwin-Westinghouse split an order for 10 similar streamlined EF-3 electrics designed for freight service. These were numbered in the 0150 series and strictly intended for AC overhead operation. As a result they were not equipped with third-rail shoes and could not run into Grand Central. The EF-3s also used a lower gearing to develop 90,000 pounds starting tractive effort, while producing 4,860 horsepower at their maximum speed of 65 miles per hour.

Great Northern's Cascade Electrics

One of the more unusual electrification projects GE undertook was Great Northern's Cascade Tunnel electrification in 1911, which used a three-phase AC system. Three-phase AC motors offer superior traction characteristics than DC motors, making them especially desirable for use on heavily graded lines. The difficulty in controlling three-phase AC motors, however, precluded wide-scale adoption of the system. Great Northern's electrics worked at 6,600 volts and required two separate sets of overhead wires to obtain three-phase current. General Electric built box-cab electrics that used four induction motors producing 1,500 horsepower. The locomotives drew current using a pair of trolley poles, one for each set of wires.

In the late 1920s, when Great Northern relocated its Cascade crossing to include the boring of a much longer Cascade Tunnel (9.1 miles in length), it replaced its three-phase electrification with a more conventional single-phase, 11,000-volt AC system, and bought new electrics from both GE and Westinghouse.

Milwaukee Road's Pacific Extension

General Electric introduced higher voltage DC electrification on interurban and suburban railway systems. The foremost example of GE's high-voltage DC system was the electrification of Milwaukee Road's fabled Pacific Extension, which ultimately consisted of more than 660 route miles of electric operation. Milwaukee's operation involved two long, but non-contiguous, sections of electrification. Inspired by GE's successful 2,400-volt DC electrification on Montana's Butte, Anaconda & Pacific, Milwaukee Road contracted GE to supply it with 3,000-volt DC overhead electrification. The railroad was keen to take advantage of cost savings afforded by its electrified operations, which began in 1915 and reached their fullest extent by 1927.

Milwaukee Road's Rocky Mountain electrification stretched 440 miles from Harlowton, Montana, to Avery, Idaho, a small, isolated village deep

Today, Milwaukee Road boxcab No. 10200, which was designated E50 in later years, is preserved and on display at the Lake Superior Railroad Museum in Duluth, Minnesota. Built by GE in 1915, this two-section boxcab was part of an order of 42 locomotives for Milwaukee's Pacific Extension electrification. When it was retired in the mid-1970s it had nearly sixty years of service behind it. *Brian Solomon*

in the Bitterroot Mountains. Milwaukee's Cascade electrification ran from Othello, Washington, over the mountains to Tacoma, and eventually Seattle.

Milwaukee's electrification was developed to satisfy different criteria than early eastern electrification programs. Milwaukee Road used electrification to lower mainline operating costs on its Pacific Extension, where the railroad faced unusual

Milwaukee Road's original GE boxcabs of 1915 were delivered in two-unit sets. Later, as the weight of trains increased, the railroad reconfigured some locomotives in to three-unit sets, such as E31 seen here at Three Forks, Montana, on June 24, 1949. With white flags flying, this gigantic electric has 119 cars in tow behind it. A few of these boxcabs survived to the end of Milwaukee's Rocky Mountain electrification in 1974. *Otto Perry, Western History Collection, Denver Public Library, OP5244*

operational circumstances. The Pacific Extension was among the last of the transcontinental mainlines, completed in 1909, 40 years after the first transcontinental railroad. Operations were especially difficult, facing prolonged 2 percent grades in the Rockies, Bitterroots, and Cascade ranges between Montana and Washington State. Where other western lines had enjoyed ample supplies of online coal, or used oil-burning steam locomotives, Milwaukee's remote operations were hampered by a lack of adjacent fuel supplies. Electric operations that harnessed hydroelectric power solved Milwaukee's fuel problems while providing

more efficient propulsion. Another benefit was the ability of electric motors to develop very high starting tractive effort, useful in ascending the railroad's grades, some of which reached 2.2 percent. Through electrification, Milwaukee was able to minimize the use of helpers and operate longer, heavier freight trains over the mountains.

Milwaukee's Bi-Polar Electrics

For Milwaukee's electric operations, GE and Alco jointly built two varieties of locomotives that appeared quite different externally. The freight locomotives were semi-permanently coupled pairs

Milwaukee Road Bi-Polar E-5 was photographed with the eastward *Olympian Hiawatha* at Seattle, Washington, on August 7, 1953. This massive articulated electric was one of five Class EP-2s built by GE for Milwaukee in 1918. These three-piece articulateds used a 1-B+D+D+B-1 wheel arrangement, and were 76 feet long and weighed more than a half-million pounds. The smoke is from the locomotive's oil-burning boiler, used to supply steam heat for passenger cars. Although this locomotive was scrapped about 1963, one of Milwaukee's Bi-Polars was preserved. *Robert A. Buck*

The Delaware, Lackawanna & Western electrified its New Jersey suburban lines in 1930 and 1931 using a 3,000-volt DC system similar to that employed by Milwaukee Road. Other than a pair of tri-power, diesel-battery-electrics similar to those used by New York Central, DL&W's electrified operations were entirely provided by multiple-units built by Pullman and powered by General Electric traction motors. Here, a four-car MU set consisting of three power cars and one trailer arrive at Denville, New Jersey, from Hoboken. *Richard Jay Solomon*

of Class EF-1 boxcabs built in 1915. These used a 2-B-B+B-B-2 arrangement, measured 112 feet long, and weighed 576,000 pounds, placing 451,000 pounds on the driving wheels. Using eight GE motors, one powering each driving axle, the boxcabs could produce 112,750 pounds tractive effort. (F. J. G. Haut, writing in *The History of the Electric Locomotive*, states a higher figure of 135,000 pounds starting tractive effort. Haut

indicates that continuous output was rated at 3,000 horsepower with a one-hour output of 3,440 horsepower.) These boxcabs were used on both electrified sections. Similar machines, designated EP-1, were initially used for passenger services on the Rocky Mountain electrified section.

In 1919, GE and Alco built five massive, three-piece articulated EP-2 electrics that were numbered E-1 to E-5 and featured an unusual

A pair of Milwaukee's Little Joes leads an eastbound freight at Harlowton, Montana, while a 1915 vintage boxcab set switches on the adjacent track. Milwaukee's electrification, heralded as the future of American railroading during World War I, was obsolete and tired by the 1970s. Although Milwaukee considered revamping its electrification, in the end it abandoned it. Electric operation ended in 1974 and in 1980 the railroad discontinued most operations west of Terry, Montana. *Mel Patrick*

On November 15, 1967, John Gruber caught South Shore Little Joe No. 802 at twilight with the headlight of an approaching passenger train on the horizon. The wires that fill the sky once represented progress to American railways. *John Gruber*

1-B-D+D-B-1 arrangement. Unlikely to be confused with any other electric ever built, these EP-2s featured a peculiar-looking center-cab configuration, articulated in three sections, with elongated and arched wagon-top hood end sections slightly lower than the cab section. Enormous headlights rode on the top of the end hoods. A General Electric Type 100 gearless, bi-polar motor powered each of the 12 driving axles; as a result, the EP-2s were commonly known as Milwaukee's *Bi-Polars*. Maximum tractive

effort figures vary, with some sources indicating 114,450 pounds. Drawing 888 amps, the Bi-Polars could deliver 42,000 pounds continuous tractive effort at 28.4 miles per hour, and produce 3,200 horsepower for traction. (One-hour output was about 10 percent higher.)

The Bi-Polars were intended to lift a 1,000-ton transcontinental passenger train up a 2 percent grade at a steady 25 miles per hour. The Bi-Polars primarily worked Milwaukee's long-distance passenger trains. E-1 was scrapped in 1961, while E-3, E-4, and E-5 survived until 1963, stored near Deer Lodge, Montana. Luckily, one of these unique machines was preserved. Today, E-2 is displayed at the Museum of Transportation in St. Louis, Missouri.

Milwaukee's mountain electrification was considered a triumph for modern technology which proponents hoped would set an example that other lines would follow. Despite its promise, the Milwaukee's electrification was an anomaly in America. While more lines embraced electrification, the percentage of electrified U. S. mainline remained very small, and where lines were electrified, high-voltage AC prevailed over GE's DC system for use on heavy overhead lines.

Different economic considerations prevailed in Europe, and today electrification is the dominant form of railway power there. While high-voltage AC systems became the most common, Belgium, Italy, Poland, and Spain adopted the 3,000-volt DC standard. Perhaps the most extensive use of DC electric traction is in Russia, where thousands of miles have been electrified.

In an interesting twist, it was an aborted Russian railway order that resulted in Milwaukee's final electric motive power acquisition. In 1947 and 1948, General Electric was filling an order for 20 double-ended, streamlined 2-D+D-2 electrics for Soviet railways when Cold War politics prevented their delivery and GE sought other buyers for its orphaned machines. With its extensive 3,000-volt electrification, Milwaukee Road was an obvious candidate, and GE lent the railroad one locomotive for testing. Because the massive locomotives were built for 5-foot Russian gauge, not the 4 feet, 8.5 inches used in the U. S., re-gauging was necessary for American operation. The type became universally known on the Milwaukee as "Little Joes," after Soviet dictator Joseph Stalin. In 1950, Milwaukee Road bought 12 of the electrics for its Rocky Mountain lines, the Indiana interurban South Shore picked up three for its 1,500-volt DC lines, and the remainder were sold to the Paulista Railway in Brazil. Milwaukee's Little Joes

operated until 1974, South Shore's until 1983. Several have been preserved, and a former South Shore machine can be seen at the Illinois Railroad Museum at Union, Illinois.

PRR Electrification Schemes

At the beginning of the twentieth century, the Pennsylvania Railroad, under the leadership of Alexander Cassatt, decided to build an underground passenger terminal in Manhattan connected with tunnels beneath the Hudson and East Rivers. The goal was a through rail route from Washington, D.C., to Boston via New York City. Cassatt had been inspired by the recently completed Gare d'Orsay in Paris, and impressed by that station's clean electric trains, which used DC third-rail traction. Experimenting with both AC overhead and DC third-rail equipment on a test track on its Long Island Rail Road subsidiary, the PRR initially chose DC for its ambitious Penn Station project. With Westinghouse as its supplier, PRR chose an over-running third rail instead of the under-running variety employed by New York Central.

In 1905, PRR's Juniata Shop in Altoona, Pennsylvania, built two experimental electrics (the Pennsy called their electric locomotives "motors," but to reduce confusion between the engine and the propulsion device, we use the conventional term in this book), numbers 10001 and 10002. The locomotives featured different traction-motor configurations, but both used the articulated B-B wheel arrangement and distributed draw-bar pull through the frame rather than the locomotive body.

The experimentals had tracking problems that led PRR engineers to both consider steam locomotive–based designs and borrow an electric locomotive from the neighboring New Haven Railroad for testing. Based on this experience PRR ordered a third experimental electric, No. 10003, from Baldwin and Westinghouse in 1907. The 70-ton, rigid-frame locomotive features 72-inch drivers in a 2-B wheel arrangement. Of the three experimentals, No. 10003 was by far the most desirable and it was used as the basis for the

The Pennsylvania Railroad used pairs of DD1 electrics like this duo at left to haul passenger trains from Pennsylvania Station in New York City, under the Hudson River, to Manhattan Transfer in New Jersey. Although these side-rod electrics may appear ponderous, they were capable of speeds up to 85 miles per hour. Pennsy GG1 No. 4900 is also seen here at Sunnyside Yard in Queens, New York. *Jim Shaughnessy*

successful DD1 design. PRR's locomotive class designation was a function of its wheel arrangement. In PRR steam locomotive terms, a Class D steam locomotive was a 4-4-0 American type; thus a DD1 was essentially two D electric locomotives back to back.

In 1909, the Juniata Shops built a DD1 prototype, No. 3998, comprising two semi-permanently coupled units, each 65 feet long, weighing 313,000 pounds, and featuring 72-inch drivers in a 2-B arrangement, such as on the 10003. Each unit was powered by a single, very powerful traction motor connected to the drivers through rods and *jackshafts*, counterweighted reciprocating parts that transfer power from the drive rod to the side rods and rods. The DD1s were designed to haul 800-ton trains of steel coaches up 1.8 percent grades in the Penn Station tunnels; the jackshaft

In the 1920s, PRR's Altoona Shops built a fleet of BB-1 and BB-2 two-unit electrics with an 0-C-0+0-C-0 wheel arrangement. Later, they were separated as single 0-C-0 units and classified B-1. Since they had the same wheel arrangement as a standard 0-6-0 steam switcher, they were ideal as electric switchers. Pennsy No. 3921 was a regular at the railroad's vast Sunnyside Yard in Queens, New York. It was photographed there on February 8, 1958. One is preserved today at the Railroad Museum of Pennsylvania at Strasburg. *Richard Jay Solomon*

arrangement allowed the use of a more powerful traction motor than could be made to fit between the locomotive's wheels.

At the time, the DD1s were among the most powerful locomotives in the world and delivered nearly 80,000 pounds of tractive effort. They were capable of 85 miles per hour, despite their ponderous appearance. Ultimately PRR built 33 DD1 pairs which handled roughly 600 daily trains into Penn Station and operated on 14 miles of third-rail mainline between Sunnyside Yard on Long Island and Manhattan Transfer, the latter a pair of isolated high-level platforms in the Jersey Meadows, with no outside access and built to allow

In preparation for its New York-to-Washington electrification, the PRR built four pairs of experimental electrics using a 2-B-2 wheel arrangement. Classed O1, O1a, O1b, and O1c, they had varied performance characteristics. PRR later decided on a slightly more powerful machine, the P5 class with a 2-C-2 wheel arrangement, making the O1 class relatively obscure. Typically they worked in pairs on light passenger trains or singly as yard engines. Here, PRR O1c No. 7857 catches the winter rays at Sunnyside Yard in February 1958; the locomotive weighed 300,000 pounds and delivered 33,500 pounds starting tractive effort. *Richard Jay Solomon*

passengers to change trains and for the railroad to exchange electric power for steam. (The station also allowed cross-platform transfer to the electrified Hudson & Manhattan Railroad—today's PATH rapid transit—for connections to lower Manhattan.)

In the late 1920s, when newer L5a electrics bumped many DD1s from trans-Hudson assignments, some were transferred to the Long Island Rail Road, where they served in commuter service for another 25 years. Interestingly, DD1 No. 36 survived into the 1960s. Often seen in Sunnyside Yard, nestled among newer electrics, the lone remaining DD1 pair was regularly assigned to wire-train service in the Penn Station tunnels. Today, this last pair is beautifully restored at the Railroad Museum of Pennsylvania in Strasburg.

PRR AC Electrification

The greater efficiency of high-voltage AC transmission over long distances made the system more attractive for large-scale mainline electrification. Although the Pennsylvania Railroad had initially committed to DC third rail for its New York terminal operations, it selected a high-voltage overhead system (based on New Haven's success) for its Philadelphia suburban services. (Penn Station's design left provisions for future overhead electrification.) In 1913, PRR inaugurated 11,000-volt, single-phase AC electrification on its Paoli and Chestnut Hill commuter routes.

PRR used a fleet of "owl eye" multiple-units (designated MP54s), so-called because of their prominent, round front windows.

The success of its Philadelphia suburban electrification led PRR to consider electrifying its rugged Allegheny Mountain grades via the famous Horseshoe Curve to Pittsburgh. Such a service would require powerful electric locomotives to haul heavy freights, so in 1917 the Juniata Shops constructed a single Class FF1 prototype, No. 3931. This monster measured 76.5 feet long, weighed 258 tons, and featured six pairs of 72-inch drivers in a 1-C+C-1 arrangement. It used

Pennsylvania Railroad MP54s clatter along the Hi Line across the Jersey Meadows from New York's Pennsylvania Station toward Newark, New Jersey, in September 1959. The MP54 design dated to 1913 and 1914 when PRR began electrifying its Philadelphia suburban lines. These Tuscan-red "owl eye" cars, powered by Westinghouse single-phase traction motors, became some of the most common sights on PRR's electrified lines. *Richard Jay Solomon*

Pennsylvania Railroad had intended to use its P5 fleet for high-speed passenger services, however problems with the locomotives resulted in PRR developing the GG1. While the P5a electrics largely worked freights in later years, on August 19, 1937, PRR P5a boxcab No. 4718 led a passenger train at Stelton, New Jersey. Today, PRR P5 boxcab No. 4700 is preserved at the Museum of Transportation in St. Louis. *Otto Perry, Western History Collection, Denver Public Library, OP14462*

Westinghouse electrical components and employed phase splitters to convert the single-phase current to three-phase AC for traction. Large induction motors powered the drive wheels via jackshafts and side rods. Although PRR eventually expanded its overhead system along several northeastern main routes, it never electrified its mountain lines and the FF1 became just one of many Pennsy locomotive curiosities.

PRR Northeast Corridor Electrification

Pennsylvania's New York–Washington, D.C., route was the primary transportation artery connecting America's largest cities. The route accommodated hundreds of daily long-distance and suburban passenger and freight trains. In 1928, Pennsylvania announced ambitious plans to electrify this busy multiple-track mainline, including a freight branch to Potomac Yards in Alexandria, Virginia.

Pennsylvania's later P5a electrics used a streamlined center-cab design and were thus designated as P5a Modified. Don't be deceived by the different appearance—internally the streamliner and the boxcab were effectively the same. Pennsylania No. 4750 was photographed with a passenger consist in Washington, D.C., on August 5, 1936. *Otto Perry, Western History Collection, Denver Public Library, OP14329*

Electrification eventually included branches, secondary mainlines, and its famous Main Line from Philadelphia to Harrisburg, Pennsylvania. Electrification allowed the railroad to speed up its services and increase line capacity without adding additional mainline tracks. According to Frederick Westing's article, "GG1" in the March 1964 issue of *TRAINS*, Westinghouse's high-power, AC traction motor design of 1927, which permitted a high-output motor to be located between main frames of a locomotive, contributed to PRR's decision to electrify. This motor changed the way PRR and others viewed electric locomotive design.

The onset of the Great Depression threatened to curtail PRR's plans but, with significant financial assistance from the federal government, PRR's New York-to-Washington mainline was opened for electric service in February 1935, and the Harrisburg electrification opened in 1939. Suburban services were largely handled by PRR's vast fleet of multiple-unit MP54s. Long-distance passenger trains, hourly "clockers" between New York and Philadelphia, heavy suburban trains, and freight were also hauled by electric locomotives.

During 1930 and 1931, PRR designed and built three new classes of electrics—L6, O1, and

The P5a was built in two body styles: a boxcab and a steeple cab, both of which are seen here hauling freight on PRR's New York–Washington electrified mainline between New Brunswick and Princeton Junction, New Jersey. In their later years, the P5/P5a electrics were the backbone of PRR's electric freight fleet. They were limited to 70 miles per hour and thus not suitable for fast passenger service. Leading is P5a No. 4735, built by Westinghouse in 1933. Some P5s were also products of General Electric or Altoona, as PRR deliberately split its orders between builders. *Tim Doherty collection, photographer unknown*

P5—applying the most successful steam locomotive wheel arrangements arranged in a dual-cab, bi-directional boxcab format. The most numerous of these were the P5 and P5a models.

Birth of the GG1

The P5 types used the 2-C-2 wheel arrangement intended to make the locomotive the electric equivalent of PRR's very successful K4s Pacific-type steam locomotive, which used the 4-6-2 arrangement (a four-wheel leading truck, six driving wheels, and two trailing wheels). Each pair of driving wheels on the P5 was powered by dual Westinghouse traction motors using a geared-quill drive.

Despite great care in their design, PRR soon found its P5 models suffered from several performance and reliability issues and deemed them inadequate for the high-speed passenger services for which they were intended. The P5 models suffered damaged axles as a result of the high torque of the twin traction motors, and in addition did not track well at high speeds. PRR reacted by placing a 70-mile-per-hour speed restriction on the P5 electrics. Although their axles were replaced, tracking problems continued. At about the same time that these technical flaws were revealed, a P5 boxcab was involved in a disastrous grade crossing accident that killed crewmembers and called into question the safety of the front-end cab design.

PRR took a proactive approach and decided to design an all-new class of electric locomotive for its premier services. First it borrowed and tested New Haven EP-3 boxcab No. 0354. The

Pennsylvania GG1 No. 4880 leads Seaboard Airline's *Silver Comet* over the Hi Line across the Jersey Meadows. This GG1 hardly strains with 18 stainless-steel passenger cars in tow. GG1 4880 was built by PRR in February 1939 with General Electric components, and was among the last GG1s in service, operating on NJ Transit suburban trains between New York Pennsylvania Station and South Amboy until 1983. It was also one of the few GG1s to retain its yellow pinstripes, long after most GG1s were adorned in the spartan Penn-Central-era black. *Richard Jay Solomon*

The Pennsylvania Railroad hired Raymond Loewy to refine the GG1's appearance. Loewy suggested using welded body construction instead of a traditional riveted body. He also introduced the five-stripe "cat whiskers" and refined details such as the marker lights with a more streamlined appearance. The result was one of the best looking locomotives of the twentieth century. GG1 No. 4859 was restored to its original Brunswick green livery with five stripes and displayed at the Harrisburg passenger station. *Brian Solomon*

A few GG1s were painted Tuscan red with five stripes to match PRR's passenger car fleet. On March 2, 1958, a red GG1 races through Harrison, New Jersey. *Richard Jay Solomon*

New Haven machine tracked well and provided an exemplary performance. In response, PRR constructed two prototypes for testing. Both were of a similar streamlined center-cab design, but featured entirely different wheel arrangements. One locomotive, Class R1, featured a 2-D-2 arrangement, essentially the same as the successful 4-8-4 Northern-type steam locomotive. The other prototype was based on the New Haven EP-3 and used the 2-C+C-2 articulated arrangement. This machine was designated as Class GG1.

Following extensive comparative testing, the GG1 design prevailed and was selected for mass production. By increasing the number of powered axles from three to six, the amount of power per axle was lowered, thus reducing the stress placed on axles. Also, where the P5 models and other electrics featured quill coupling to just one driving wheel per axle, the GG1 had both driving wheels coupled. In the initial design, the quill engaged each wheel using six sets of spring cups. A pair of motors continuously rated at 385 horsepower powered each axle. With 12 traction motors, the GG1 could produce 4,680 continuous horsepower, and as much as 10,000 horsepower in short bursts. This enormous power potential gave the GG1 great pulling power and superb acceleration. In service,

most GG1s were rated for 100-mile-per-hour operation. In tests, however, they were capable of much faster speeds.

Before the GG1 entered regular production, PRR hired industrial designer Raymond Loewy to refine the locomotive's appearance. Loewy was the most respected man in his field, practically having invented the profession of industrial design. Although often solely credited with the GG1's characteristic shape, Loewy was not responsible for the basic design, but rather for its perfection. His refinements included the use of a seamless welded skin instead of the crude riveted skin used on the prototype, and the design of the classic five-stripe "cat whiskers" paint scheme that would later be adopted as PRR's primary passenger diesel scheme.

Between 1935 and 1943, PRR took delivery of a fleet of 138 production GG1s. Along with the 1934 prototype, they were numbered from 4800 to 4938. The GG1s were not the product of one builder. Some of the locomotives were built at the railway's renowned Altoona Shops, where many of PRR's steam locomotives were also built, while others were built by Baldwin and General Electric. Although they used electrical components from both Westinghouse and General Electric, and were erected at three different locations, the GG1s were of a standard design. There were some minor differences in weight and tractive effort from locomotive to locomotive, and the typical machine weighed 477,000 pounds with about 303,000 pounds on drivers, and with a 24:77 gear ratio delivering 70,700 pounds starting tractive effort based on 25 percent adhesion.

Initially, the GG1s were primarily assigned to premier passenger runs. When PRR began retiring many of its older boxcabs in the 1950s and early 1960s, a number of them were bumped into freight service. Following the Penn-Central merger of 1968, the bulk of the GG1s were given a non-attractive, utilitarian black paint scheme. After the absorption of the bankrupt New Haven Railroad into Penn-Central in 1969, GG1s ran past New York City on a regular basis for the first time and became regular power to New Haven. When Amtrak was created in 1971, it inherited a number of GG1s for service on the New Haven-to-Washington, D.C., Northeast Corridor. Ten years later they were finally superseded by a more modern locomotive, the Swedish inspired AEM-7.

In 1976, Conrail assumed the freight operations of several bankrupt northeastern railways, including Penn-Central, and gained a number of freight-service GG1s, along with other former PRR, New York Central, and New Haven electric locomotives. The last few active fleets of GG1s were assigned to the New Jersey Department of Transportation (later NJ Transit), operating on New York & Long Branch suburban trains between South Amboy, New Jersey, and Pennsylvania Station, New York. Finally, on October 29, 1983, after nearly 50 years of continuous service, a GG1 lowered its pantograph for the last time. Today, several are preserved in railway museums around the country.

In 1938, PRR built a prototype DD2 overhead AC electric with a 2-B+B-2 wheel arrangement and styling that resembled a short, bloated GG1. This 5,000-horsepower experimental was intended for the electrification of the PRR mainline between Harrisburg and Pittsburgh over the Alleghenies, which was deferred and then later cancelled, first due to World War II, and later because of the advent of diesel-electric technology.

Although *TRAINS* magazine forewarned the GG1's ultimate demise in the mid-1960s, many of the old electrics soldiered on through the 1970s. Amtrak retired its last GG1s in 1981, and the final 13 GG1s were operated by NJ Transit between Pennsylvania Station, New York, and South Amboy, New Jersey, until October 1983. A year before its retirement, GG1 No. 4883 was photographed under wire at the South Amboy engine terminal. *Brian Solomon*

A RIDE ON A G

BY RICHARD JAY SOLOMON

One night some 40-plus years ago, I was attending a very boring business meeting of a New York railroad enthusiasts' society, which fortunately took place in the old Penn Station YMCA, upstairs in the Eighth Avenue office wing. When things got too tedious, members would wander down to the tracks to observe real trains. Sometimes, interesting things would transpire.

This evening I had with me my brand new Rolleiflex T, loaded with black-and-white film, and a tripod, with the thought that I might take a few night shots if the opportunity presented. A few minutes into the irrelevant debate, a friend and I found ourselves on the platforms several stories below the meeting room, photographing GG1 No. 4892 on the point of a PRR commuter train heading for the Jersey Shore.

It's the early 1960s, and a GG1 locomotive crew consults with their conductor at Penn Station, New York. Minutes after this photo was taken, the photographer was invited into the cab of the locomotive and experienced the thrill of a cab ride through the Penn tunnels, down the PRR mainline to Rahway Junction, and then on to the New York & Long Branch to South Amboy, New Jersey. Richard Jay Solomon

We set up the tripod at the far western end of the station, on one of the extra-lengthy platforms intended for long Florida and western sleeper consists, and with no vertical bents to obstruct the view. It's hard to imagine today how relaxed railroad employees were back then, despite the height of Cold War paranoia. As luck would have it, 4892's engineer asked, "You guys like a ride?" Do steel wheels have flanges? The tripod seemed to fold itself, and in a flash we hopped into the cab.

This wasn't my first cab ride, but it was my first inside an electric locomotive, and Raymond Loewy's masterpiece, to boot—my favorite engine since my childhood Lionel days. I first saw a real GG1 when my father took me along on a business trip to Philadelphia at age 11. We arrived at the old Broad Street stub-end station and debarked onto its track-level platform, where I got to see a G from the wheels up. My first impression was how much longer the real loco was than my Lionel version. Its wheels were greater in diameter than I was tall. And its cooling fans were really, really loud.

Since that early encounter, I had closely examined electrics in yards and stations on two continents, and shot them on high-speed mainlines, but anticipating this ride still brought a thrill. I positioned myself behind the engineer on the right side, watching the cab-signal bar. My friend stood behind the fireman. I attempted handheld photos, but the slow speed of contemporary film, and the rather dim illumination from Penn Station's original low-wattage incandescents, obviated any decent cab shots. We slowly clacked our way across the Tenth Avenue yard ladder, under the emergency river gates installed during World War II to prevent flooding by enemy torpedoes, and then rapidly picked up speed as our short commuter train accelerated downhill under the river. We roared out of the Bergen portals into the Jersey Meadows at better than 70 miles per hour. Surrounded by the massive bulk of the locomotive, it was not at all like riding in the front of an MU onto the highline.

Inside the cab, the GG1 seemed even larger than it did from outside. It struck me that the Pennsy's safety design, putting the cab in the center, protected by its heavy electrical equipment, wasn't much different than that of a large steam engine with its boiler and firebox ahead of the cab to protect the crew from head-on mishaps. Riding behind the electric's engineer, I had the same feeling I had the previous year when I rode behind the fireman on a Norfolk & Western steam engine switching at Roanoke: The GG1's gigantic, if streamlined, nose gave the same impression as a gigantic boiler, sans the hiss, heat, and smoke.

We ran express from Newark to Perth Amboy, uncoupling and running around the train at the next stop, South Amboy, the end of electrification on the PRR's New York and Long Branch subsidiary. We observed a Baldwin sharknose diesel being hooked onto the train for Bay Head Junction, while we prepared to head back to New York running light, pantographs now reversed.

While the engineer and fireman climbed down to check running gear, they told us to just walk alongside the motors, racks of rather hot equipment and roaring fans, from one cab to the other. "Better that way so no one sees you," was the hint we really shouldn't be there. Light engines, with nothing in tow, had restricted top speeds to prevent derailment, but the engine crew was anxious to return home. We flew up the branch and mainline at better than 90 miles per hour, slowing slightly and giving a couple of honks of the airhorn as we passed the high-level platforms at Newark. We left a train of Hudson & Manhattan "black" cars at Harrison in the dust, and got back up to full speed on the highline across the Meadows, zipping past speeders on the Jersey Turnpike before enetering the Hudson tunnels. We stopped at the easternmost end of Penn Station, the engineer telling us to "Get off here where no one will see you. We're heading to Sunnyside, but you'd be seen there climbing down the ladder and just might get me into trouble." We hopped back onto the high-level platform and thanked the crew profusely, but they really didn't want to give us their names—anonymity has its benefits.

"Where have *you* been?" we were asked back up at the meeting, some three hours after we left. "You missed a real exciting debate!"

"Really? Well, we just had a roundtrip in a G's cab, to and from South Amboy."

"Sure, you did," came the reply. But I have my photos—and I can still smell the ozone.

On August 13, 1959, GG1 No. 4934 emerges from the East River Tunnels at Sunnyside Yard in Queens. A GG1 drew current from 11,000-volt, 25Hz catenary and used an onboard transformer to step down the voltage for use by 12 single-phase AC traction motors. The GG1s were capable of rapid acceleration and could singly haul a twenty-car train at 100 miles per hour without difficulty. While its continuous rating was 4,620 horsepower, a GG1 could produce as much as 10,000 horsepower in short spurts. Richard Jay Solomon

ELECTROLINER DESIGN

BY JOHN GRUBER

The North Shore Line introduced its high-speed streamlined articulated *Electroliners* in 1941 in a fashion befitting a main line steam road. The speedy Chicago-to-Milwaukee electric interurban railroad, which advertised "every hour on the hour" service, had commissioned James F. Eppenstein, a Chicago architect, to style its two four-unit articulated trains from top to bottom, inside and out.

Eppenstein (1899–1955) had worked at his father's factory in Elgin, Illinois, from 1919 to 1928, but always wanted to be an architect. He returned to college in the U. S. and Europe and opened his architecture firm in Chicago in 1934.

Albert L. Arenberg, president of Luminator Company, whose innovative lighting fixtures locomotive designers began using in the 1930s, introduced Eppenstein

The Chicago, North Shore & Milwaukee interurban electric line offered high-speed passenger services between its namesake cities. In 1941, it placed two new streamlined articulated electric trains in service. After North Shore ceased operations in 1963, the trains were bought by Philadelphia's Red Arrow Lines, where they served as Liberty Liners. Richard Jay Solomon

to North Shore officials. Arenberg's son, Henry, recalls, "Before the first meeting, my father had Jim in his office. 'Where's your hat?' my father asked Jim, who had this beautiful head of hair, very well done. Jim did not own a hat. Since you had to have a hat to do business with a railroad, my father went out to buy Jim a hat and together they went to the NS offices." Eppenstein won the styling contract and Arenberg the lighting contract.

The North Shore and Eppenstein started out by carefully examining passenger traffic. "Inasmuch as these trains are used very largely for commuting service between the various cities on the line, it is natural that a very large percentage of the passengers should be women. It was therefore felt that the interiors should be unusually inviting, in order to appeal to feminine tastes," reported *Mass Transportation* magazine.

Each car had a different interior color scheme. Floor patterns and colors also were different. "It was also felt that there should be as large a variety as possible in the appearance of the various cars in order that the passengers who make the frequent trips on the trains should have an opportunity to enjoy different surroundings," the magazine continued. Most of the murals above the windows were "amusing and all of them pleasant and colorful."

"These murals reach their height in gaiety in the Tavern Car where they consist of various brightly colored animals engaged in a variety of activities—for instance, a pink elephant walking a tight rope," according to the *Mass Transportation* article. "Here in the Tavern Car also are deep luxurious seats of a new type, designed by James Eppenstein and Associates, and not before used in transportation equipment."

Eppenstein's exterior—jade green for the body of the cars with brilliant red-orange stripes—was designed "to give the impression of high speed even when the train is at rest."

Although the trains could not match the Chicago-to-Milwaukee timing of Milwaukee Road's famous *Hiawathas* or Chicago & North Western's *400s*, North Shore's *Electroliners* turned in amazing performances. The pair of trains made five round trips daily, covering the 88 miles between Adams and Wabash in Chicago to North Shore's Milwaukee Terminal in just 1 hour and 54 minutes. This included 10 intermediate stops, 11 miles of the Chicago elevated, and 3 miles on Milwaukee streets.

Eppenstein later did other railway-related work, providing the paint scheme for Chicago Rapid Transit's 5000-series aluminum articulated train sets (two built by Pullman, two by St. Louis Car) introduced in 1945.

Both *Electroliners* survive today, one at the Illinois Railroad Museum in Union, Illinois, the other at Orbsonia, Pennsylvania—a tribute to their well-deserved place in the history of electric railroading.

Note: John Horachek, a conductor on the last Electroliner *into Milwaukee in 1963, assisted with information about Eppenstein and styling. Horachek is a member of the North Shore Reunion Committee, which coordinates the annual event in Waukegan, Illinois.*

A pair of freshly shopped EF-4 electrics leads a freight at Fresh Pond Junction in Queens in the autumn of 1964. New Haven was the third owner of these Ignitron (mercury-arc) rectifiers, having bought them from Norfolk & Western after the latter line discontinued electric operations inherited from the Virginian. *Richard Jay Solomon*

CHAPTER 2

AC RECTIFIERS

AC-DC Converter Locomotives

High-voltage, single-phase AC transmission had become the predominant choice for railroad electrification by the 1930s. In addition to the New Haven and Pennsylvania, the Boston & Maine, Virginian, and Norfolk & Western adopted 11,000-volt AC.

In the early years, AC electrified lines employed transformer locomotives that reduced line current to a lower voltage for use by single-phase AC traction motors. Norfolk & Western, and later Virginian, employed locomotives with phase splitters (like that on the Pennsy FF1 prototype; see Chapter 1) to convert single-phase current to three-phase for use by synchronous induction motors. Power was transmitted from motors to drive wheels using jackshafts and side rods. Three-phase motors permitted exceptionally high starting tractive effort desired for moving heavy-load coal trains over the Appalachians. Since AC-induction motors have constant-speed characteristics, various pole arrangements were provided for different running speeds.

By the mid-1920s, advances in electric technology resulted in the construction of hybrid locomotives that converted single-phase AC power to DC power, allowing high-voltage AC locomotives to use DC traction motors that provided superior railway traction characteristics. Between 1926 and 1930, Baldwin-Westinghouse and Alco-GE built several classes of AC-DC converter locomotives for Great Northern to replace three-phase electrics when GN re-electrified its Cascade crossing.

One half of two-piece EL-2B electric No. 126 rests at Virginian's Princeton, West Virginia, shops in July 1958. General Electric custom-built four EL-2B motor-generator electrics for Virginian in 1948. These massive machines were designed for a top speed of 50 miles per hour, and a matched pair delivered 6,800 horsepower using a B-B+B-B + B-B+B-B wheel arrangement. Virginian had a long history of buying extremely powerful specialized locomotives for coal service. *Richard Jay Solomon*

By the end of World War II, diesel-electric development had perfected locomotive trucks and nose-suspended DC traction motors for heavy railroad service and high-speed operation. New truck designs allowed diesels to operate at speeds of more than 100 miles per hour without tracking difficulties, enabling nose-suspended DC motors powering bogie-trucks to effectively supercede the use of AC single-phase series commutator motors in new straight electrics. As a result, for the postwar market, new electrics were built using standard nose-suspended traction-motor types and diesel-like trucks. This obviated cumbersome steam-era wheel arrangements with unpowered axles. However, electrics continued to use specialized wheel arrangements in order to apply more power to the rails than possible with standard diesel-electrics. Single-unit electrics were still vastly more powerful than diesel-electric models.

In 1946, Alco-GE built a pair of gigantic, streamlined motor-generator electrics for Great Northern measuring 101 feet long, weighing

735,000 pounds, and employing a B-D+D-B wheel arrangement. All axles were powered. Transformers converted line voltage from 11,000 volts AC to 1,350 volts AC. This current was used to turn a pair of DC generators, which in turn fed power to 12 GE 746 nose-suspended traction motors, one powering each axle using a 17:70 gear ratio. They produced 5,000 horsepower and developed 183,750 pounds starting tractive effort and 119,000 pounds continuous tractive effort at just over 15 miles per hour.

Using the same technology, GE built two pairs of semi-permanently coupled streamlined AC-DC motor-generator electrics for Virginian in 1948. Numbered 125 to 128 (each unit had its own number), these modern AC-DC electrics were needed to augment Virginian's side-rodders, which by then were more than twenty years old. Although split-phase ACs were considered Virginian's best choice in 1925, by the mid-1940s, three-phase AC traction had fallen out of favor. Virginian's big GE's were classed EL-2B, and each employed a B-B+B-B wheel arrangement. According to *The Virginian Railway* by H. Reid, a mated pair weighed 1,033,832 pounds, delivered 260,000 pounds starting tractive effort, and produced 6,800 horsepower with a maximum speed of 50 miles per hour.

Mercury-Arc Rectifiers

Mercury-arc rectifier technology had been studied for railway locomotive applications since World War I. Articles in *The Railway Gazette* during the 1930s promoted this technology for AC-DC locomotives, but mercury-arc rectification was not yet sufficiently rugged for railway applications. During World War II, advances in this technology finally made the development of high-voltage AC-DC rectifier locomotives possible, and within a few years mercury-arc technology superceded the need for new motor-generator locomotives.

In the early 1950s, PRR ordered several experimental electrics in preparation of replacing its fleets of O1, L6, and P5 models, locomotives that were approaching two decades of heavy service and

In 1951, Baldwin-Westinghouse built two pairs of mercury-arc rectifiers for the Pennsylvania Railroad. One pair used C-C trucks and was classed E3b, while the other, pictured here at Meadows Yard near Kearny, New Jersey, on May 10, 1959, rode on three four-axle trucks in an unusual B-B-B wheel arrangement. Equipped with Westinghouse Type 370 DC traction motors, these machines were extremely powerful. A pair delivered 189,000 pounds starting tractive effort and 132,000 pounds continuous tractive effort at 17 miles per hour. *Richard Jay Solomon*

which had never lived up to expectations. Westinghouse built two types of Ignitron-tube rectifier locomotives for PRR. Ignitron rectification was a variation of the mercury-arc technology deemed suitable for heavy railroad applications. Ignitron tubes were used to convert alternating current to pulsating direct current, which was then passed through reactors to smooth it for use by traction motors. According to "Pennsy's New Juice Jacks," published in the February 1954 issue of *TRAINS*, each tube measured 3 feet tall and 9 inches in diameter. A pool of mercury was located at the base of the tube with an igniter resting in it. At the top of the tube

New Haven's last order for suburban-service multiple-units consisted of 100 cars built by Pullman-Standard in 1954. They used Ignitron rectifier tubes to convert 11,000-volt AC current to 600-volt DC current for traction motors, and like other New Haven passenger equipment they had third-rail shoes for operation into Grand Central. In October 1963, a set of these MUs, colloquially known as "Washboards," make a station stop at Riverside, Connecticut. *Richard Jay Solomon*

was a carbon anode, an arrangement that only permitted the passage of current in one direction. A water circuit was used to keep the tubes cool.

Westinghouse built two E3b electrics, Nos. 4995 and 4996, which used an unusual B-B-B wheel arrangement, and two E2c electrics, Nos. 4997 and 4998, which rode on C-C trucks. Both types had a streamlined cab design similar to carbody diesels of the period. Each of the three units was rated at 3,000 horsepower and delivered 94,500 pounds maximum tractive effort. General Electric built three pairs of experimental locomotives, class E2b,

which used essentially the same technology perfected for the GG1 electrics. These locomotives resembled Alco-GE FA diesel-electrics, and each pair produced 5,000 horsepower, or 2,500 horsepower per unit. The experimentals spent several years hauling freights on PRR while the railroad analyzed their performance.

New Haven was among the first lines to purchase Ignitron-rectifier electrics for regular service, ordering a fleet of 100 multiple-unit passenger cars with Ignitron rectifiers from Pullman-Standard in 1954. Later it took delivery of ten Class EP5

New Haven EP5 No. 378 leads an eastbound passenger train at Stamford, Connecticut, on June 29, 1958. New Haven's EP5 electrics regularly worked long-distance passenger trains between New Haven, Connecticut, and both Grand Central Terminal and Pennsylvania Station. After New Haven was absorbed by Penn-Central, the EP5s were reassigned to freight service and were retired shortly after Conrail assumed operations of Penn-Central in 1976. *Richard Jay Solomon*

The General Electric–built E2b featured an array of MU connectors to allow operation with various other electrics. According to author Michael Bezilla, Pennsylvania Railroad was not impressed by motor-generator locomotives, preferring straight AC types. Transformers were used to reduce the current and supply four Type GEA-632 traction motors on each locomotive. A pair of E2bs delivered 122,750 pounds starting tractive effort. *Richard Jay Solomon*

streamlined, double-ended Ignitron-rectifier passenger electrics from GE. The EP5 electrics measured 68 feet long and weighed 348,000 pounds. They were New Haven's most powerful passenger electrics, delivering 87,000 pounds starting tractive effort and producing 4,000 horsepower. By comparison, the EP-2s of 1919–1927 were rated at 2,050 horsepower, and the EP-4s at 3,600 horsepower.

The EP5 electrics were substantially more powerful than any single-unit diesel-electric built at that time, yet shared many common characteristics with contemporary diesels. Like PRR's E2b electrics built a few years earlier, they shared styling with Alco-GE diesel-electrics, and had nose-

suspended traction motors similar to those used by contemporary Alco-GE diesel-electrics.

During the mid-1950s, New Haven scaled back its electric operations. Much of its physical plant was nearly worn out after five decades of heavy use. It substituted diesels for electrics in its yards, and eliminated electric freight operations for a few years. Instead of buying more EP5 electrics, it invested in a unique fleet of 60 dual-mode diesel-electric/third-rail electrics built by the Electro-Motive Division of General Motors. The FL9s operated as standard diesel-electrics outside of third-rail territory, but featured reversible shoes to draw current from both New York Central's

At Woodlawn Junction in The Bronx, New Haven electrics switched from overhead AC power to third-rail DC power while at speed. Heading toward Grand Central, EP5 No. 375 has nearly reached the end of the overhead electrification at Woodlawn on October 17, 1959. Its pantograph has been lowered and its third-rail shoes are ready to start drawing current. Passengers on board the train will be oblivious to the change in power. *Richard Jay Solomon*

under-running and PRR's over-running third rails, allowing them to operate on through runs between Boston's South Station Boston and Manhattan's Grand Central and Penn stations. The FL9s replaced many of New Haven's older passenger electrics and its World War II–era fleet of Alco DL109 diesel-electrics.

According to Jerry Pinkepank in a 1964 *TRAINS* magazine article, the cost of a new FL9 was half that of an EP5, and the EP5 models had relatively short careers compared to both New Haven's EP-1s and the FL9s. Whereas the latter two types served for four decades, the EP5

electrics barely lasted two. Following New Haven's inclusion in Penn-Central in 1969, the EP5s were bumped off passenger assignments. A few worked in freight up to the advent of Conrail, and all were scrapped by the late 1970s.

In 1955, the Virginian ordered a dozen Ignitron rectifiers from GE to finally replace its three-phase, side-rod electrics in heavy coal service. Designated EL-C, the GE rectifiers were delivered over the next two years. They were much like contemporary high-output diesels and were among the first modern electrics to use the road-switcher configuration. Like New Haven's EP5

On the afternoon of July 1, 1958, a pair of New Haven's dual-mode FL9s leads a Grand Central–bound train over New York Central's Harlem Division at Williamsbridge in The Bronx. In the distance, two New York City Transit (IRT Division) rapid transit trains pass on the since-removed Third Avenue elevated connection to the White Plains Road Line. Shortly after 1900, the elevated railways were electrified using an over-running third rail, greatly influencing New York Central's decision to select DC third rail, although it chose an under-running variety for safety reasons. *Richard Jay Solomon*

electrics, they used C-C trucks and were powered by nose-suspended traction motors. Each unit weighed 348,000 pounds, delivered 98,500 pounds maximum tractive effort, and produced 3,300 horsepower.

Virginian often assigned them in sets of twos and threes to its exceptionally heavy coal trains. Their stint in coal service was exceptionally brief. In 1959, the company was bought by Norfolk & Western, which had discontinued their own electrification in 1950. N&W aimed to consolidate the railroads' parallel mainlines and effectively turned the Virginian route into a single-direction railroad.

Under this scheme, the Virginian's electrification had little function and was discontinued in 1962. Its 12 nearly new Ignitron electrics were sold to New Haven in 1963. New Haven classed them EF-4, repainted them in an orange-and-white livery, and used them to reintroduce electric freight service between New York City's Brooklyn Bay Ridge yards and New Haven, Connecticut. Some of the EF-4s survived into the Conrail era, giving the electrics five different owners in their two-decade-long careers. Today, Virginian No. 133 is preserved at the Virginia Museum of Transportation in Roanoke.

Pennsy's E44s

Pleased with the experimental E2c electrics, PRR ordered a fleet of high-horsepower Ignitron-rectifier electrics from GE in 1959. These used a C-C road-switcher configuration similar to that on

Pennsylvania Railroad E44 No. 4427 leads a freight along the Northeast Corridor near Morrisville, Pennsylvania, in June 1963. Since the E44s were rated at 4,400 horsepower, they were nearly twice as powerful as contemporary diesel-electrics, and were often used singly as well as in multiple. *Richard Jay Solomon*

Left: Virginian EL-C rectifier electric No. 137, built by General Electric in December 1956, is pictured at Princeton, West Virginia, on July 29, 1958. Most of Virginian's six-motor electrics served five owners. They were classified as EF-4s by New Haven, and as E33s by Penn-Central and Conrail, the latter designation reflecting their 3,300-horsepower output. They were retired by Conrail in the early 1980s. *Richard Jay Solomon*

the Virginian's EL-Cs. PRR's machines were designated E44 (for "Electric 4400" horsepower) and measured 69 feet, 6 inches long and weighed 386,000 pounds. The E44 propulsion system used a main transformer to supply a dozen Ignitron tubes that converted the current to DC for six GE Model 752 E5 traction motors. The 752 model, a series-wound DC motor, was

A pair of E44s with a caboose (or *cabin,* in PRR lexicon) runs *cab hop* along the Northeast Corridor in the vicinity of Edison, New Jersey, in June 1963. The E44s were the last new electrics built for the Pennsylvania. *Richard Jay Solomon*

the standard nose-suspended motor used to power the vast majority of GE's DC-traction diesel-electrics from the early 1960s onward.

A total of 66 E44s were built for PRR. During their production, advances in solid-state technology produced silicon diodes for use in high-voltage rectification. These air-cooled devices are simpler and require less maintenance than Ignitron tubes, and they quickly made the older technology obsolete. The last E44s were built with air-cooled, silicon-diode rectifiers, designated E44A, and used a different gearing and variation of the 752 traction motor. The result was slightly more powerful, producing an additional 600 horsepower and higher top speeds. A few early E44s were upgraded to E44A specs and by the late 1960s the entire fleet had been converted to silicon-diode rectification.

The E44/E44As, along with members of the GG1 fleet, handled PRR electric freight operations until the Penn-Central merger. Following the financial collapse of Penn-Central, early in the Conrail era, electric freight operations were discontinued. By 1981, most of the E44s were stored at Enola Yards near Harrisburg, Pennsylvania. While Conrail briefly experimented with a modified E44 in the mid-1980s, changes in its traffic patterns and freight routing, in part a reaction to high fees charged to use the Amtrak-controlled Northeast Corridor, precluded Conrail's return to electric freight operations.

E60 Electrics

In the early 1970s, Amtrak—recently created by the federal government to relieve ailing freight railroads of the burden of revenue-losing passenger services—sought new electrics to replace their inherited fleet of aged PRR GG1s. Amtrak contracted with GE to build a fleet of 26 double-ended, high-horsepower E60CP/E60CH electrics

Typically, E60s have been used to haul long-distance Northeast Corridor passenger trains that would be too heavy for a single AEM-7. On October 25, 1991, E60 No. 607 hauls a Florida-bound train past an industrial landscape near Marcus Hook, Pennsylvania. *Brian Solomon*

for high-speed passenger services. The E60CP featured a steam generator to provide heat and lighting for traditional passenger equipment; the E60CHs were equipped with more modern head-end electric power for heat and electricity. According to *The Contemporary Diesel Spotter's Guide* by Louis Marre and Jerry Pinkepank, Amtrak's locomotives were based on a single-ended freight locomotive designated E60C for the Black Mesa & Lake Powell line in Arizona, an off-network,

non-common carrier built to haul coal to regional generating stations. Amtrak's E60CP/E60CHs were unadorned, flat-fronted machines, dressed in its red-blue-and-silver scheme. These spartan-looking machines produced 6,000 horsepower output and delivered 75,000 pounds starting tractive effort. Although intended for 120-mile-per-hour service, E60CP/E60CHs suffered from a flawed truck design and were later relegated to a maximum speed of 85 miles per hour.

Amtrak E60 No. 604 leads train No. 629 passed Harrison, New Jersey, at 5:59 P.M. on August 15, 2000. At this location, the outside tracks are used by PATH, a third-rail rapid transit line once owned by the Pennsylvania Railroad, which connects Newark, New Jersey, with Manhattan. *Patrick Yough*

Amtrak sought a more effective high-speed locomotive, and ultimately settled on a derivative of the highly successful Swedish Rc4 type. Following the arrival of the AEM-7s (see Chapter 3) in the early 1980s, Amtrak sold some of its E60s to suburban passenger operator NJ Transit and to the Navajo Mine, a mining railway in New Mexico, however several were retained by Amtrak

and remained in regular passenger service. In later years, E60s have been used on heavy long-distance trains that traverse the Northeast Corridor between New York and Washington, D.C. In the early 1980s, GE built a pair of E60C-2s for the Deseret Western, a 35-mile-long coal railway in Colorado and Utah, as well as similar types for export.

A pair of AEM-7s leads a New York–bound Amtrak train at Grace interlocking, Havre de Grace, Maryland, on October 23, 1992. The AEM-7 was Amtrak's standard electric for the better part of two decades. Pairs were routinely assigned to trains with more than eight cars. *Brian Solomon*

CHAPTER 3

MODERN ELECTRICS

Diesels versus Electrics

For decades, American railroads eyed electrification cautiously, carefully weighing the advantages of straight-electric operations against the high costs of electrifying their lines. In his book, *From Bullets to BART,* William D. Middleton points out that "in 1938, America led the world in railroad electrification." Yet, from that point onward, very little new mainline electrification was undertaken in the United States. Following World War II, American railroads favored large-scale dieselization and, in the two decades from 1940 to 1960, rapidly dispensed with their steam locomotive fleets in favor of new diesels. During this steam-to-diesel transition period, many railroads that had experimented with electrification discontinued their electric operations. Boston & Maine ceased its Hoosac Tunnel electrification in 1946. Great Northern ended its Cascade Tunnel electrification in 1956. Even the New Haven scaled back its electrification in the 1950s and 1960s in favor of diesels.

Diesel-electrics have most of the advantages of straight electrics while providing greater operational flexibility. Railroads found little cost incentive to maintain separate fleets of electric locomotives, and saw extension of electric operations as cost prohibitive.

Short-term economics were a dominant consideration in switching from steam to another power source. Pennsylvania Railroad's 1930s electrification had benefited from government loans to offset the high costs

New Haven's original triangular catenary had been in service for nearly eight decades when this photo of Amtrak No. 926 was made at Port Chester, New York, on August 13, 1987. While the New Haven adopted conventional compound catenary for its later electrification schemes, its unusual triangular catenary remained on the Woodlawn Junction-to-Stamford section and was only replaced in the last few years. *Brian Solomon*

of implementation. Furthermore, advances in diesel technology closed the gap between diesel-electric and straight electric performance. In 1945, a standard single-unit freight diesel was rated between 1,000 and 1,350 horsepower; by 1966, 3,000 horsepower was standard. Improvements in the electrical components used by diesels increased tractive effort characteristics and improved reliability.

While modern electrics still offer superior performance and efficiency, today the most modern single-unit diesel-electrics are rated between 4,400 and 6,000 horsepower and, with modern three-phase traction systems, can deliver tractive effort in excess of 150,000 pounds.

In Europe, the situation has been viewed differently and has followed a divergent developmental course. In the postwar environment, European railways were state-run institutions and operated as strategic national infrastructure. As such, they have enjoyed the benefits of long-term strategic planning, large subsidies, and public investment. Where America focused its public transport investment on its Interstate highway system in the 1950s and 1960s, European countries invested heavily in railways, including wide-scale electrification. Unlike America's privately owned railroads, Europe's publicly owned and operated lines do not suffer from a greater tax burden when they undergo upgrades, which American governing bodies see as taxable improvements to privately run property. And because fossil fuels in Europe cost three to five times more than in the United States, European countries without substantial oil reserves have more incentive to invest in transportation infrastructures and take advantage of centralized forms of power, such as nuclear and hydro.

The operational differences between European and American railways also affect decisions regarding electrification. American railroads have long relied on freight traffic for the majority of their revenue. Greater distances combined with a desire to lower labor costs led American railroads to seek cost advantages by running long and

In order to reduce smoke emissions, Illinois Central was compelled by the city of Chicago to electrify its intensive suburban services. IC electric services began in 1926 using a 1,500-volt DC overhead system. A pair of IC's original MU cars, built in the 1920s, works the South Chicago branch in the early 1960s. *Richard Jay Solomon*

heavy freight trains. In Europe, passenger traffic is dominant, and mainline railway operations have tended toward short frequent train services. Since networks have developed around the operation of relatively short passenger trains, freight trains have also tended to be much shorter and lighter than those operated in the United States. Also, since frequent operations are best suited to passenger operations, and in the post–World War II market American railroads suffered from rapid declines in passenger revenue, few lines were interested in making large, long-term investments in money-losing traffic.

In the 1910s and 1920s, the situation had been different, and many suburban railways elected for electrification. As the diesel invaded freight operations, American electrified passenger lines, including those of the New Haven, Pennsylvania, New York Central, Long Island, Illinois Central, Lackawanna, and Reading, found it in their best interests to maintain existing electric systems for heavy suburban traffic. The majority of these electric services have been provided with electric MUs rather than locomotive-hauled services, although today electric locomotives with push-pull consists have found favor on some heavy suburban runs.

By the early 1980s, the remaining American electrified mainline operations were almost exclusively passenger services. Milwaukee Road discontinued its last electric operations in 1974, and Conrail, which had assumed operation of freight services on former Pennsylvania and New Haven railroad lines, discontinued electric operations by 1981. A few isolated mineral lines, such as the Deseret Western in Utah, introduced electric operations, but they are not representative of typical American heavy-haul freight operations.

European Electrics in America

The massive investment in the electrification of European railways spurred intensive research and development by European locomotive manufacturers, electrical supply companies, and government research laboratories. European firms such as ASEA, Alstom, and Siemens had direct access to substantial markets for new electric locomotives, making the investment worthwhile. From the 1960s onward, American firms, such as General Electric and General Motors, by contrast, emphasized the perfection and production of diesel-electrics. As a result, American manufacturers have led the way in diesel-electric technology, while advanced electric locomotive design has been the domain of European and Japanese builders.

Although GE continued to build electric locomotives through the 1970s and 1980s, low demand, combined with competition from more advanced

European designs, resulted in only a handful of electrics for domestic services. Today, the American market for electrics is dominated by European designs typically manufactured domestically, or in Canada under contract.

AEM-7

In the mid-1970s, following the unsuccessful experiences with E60s in high-speed service, Amtrak imported French electric No. 21003 and a Swedish State Railways (Staten Järnväger or SJ) Rc4 electric for tests on the Northeast Corridor. The Rc4 was the latest in the Rc series, built by Allmänna Svenska Elektriska Aktiebolag (ASEA) and considered one of the best locomotives on the market. The Rc type was developed in the 1960s as a dual-service electric and was the first commercial locomotive to employ thyristor motor control. Thyristors are semiconductors that represent an electronic advancement over traditional electromechanical or pneumatic motor controls. They provide stepless traction motor regulation, allowing for maximum motor output without wheel slip. This gives a locomotive greater tractive effort with improved efficiency over early systems.

Variations of the Rc type have been employed in more than a half-dozen nations, from Sweden to Bulgaria. In Sweden, overhead catenary is energized at 15,000 volts at 16.6Hz. While there are some differences between the various Rc models, the majority of SJ's Rc types were designed for 4,555 horsepower continuous output and assigned to both freight and passenger services. Traditionally, the maximum speed of Rc types was 84 miles per hour, though since the 1980s some Rc types have been geared for 100-mile-per-hour operations.

The American AEM-7 is derived from the Swedish Rc electrics and built under license in the United States. Here, a pair of Rcs races northward with a Green Cargo intermodal train at Kiruna, Sweden, in July 2002. Amtrak's AEM-7 is heavier and designed for faster service then the Rc types. *Brian Solomon*

Rc6 No. 18, lettered for the Swedish Tågkompaniet (Train Company), a private passenger train operator, pauses with a local passenger train at Kiruna, Sweden, in the twilight glow of a late summer evening. *Brian Solomon*

Amtrak demands were somewhat different than those of SJ, and the variant designed for Amtrak was intended strictly for high-speed passenger service, capable of regular operations at 125 miles per hour. The newly designed machine, designated AEM-7, was built by General Motors' Electro-Motive Division at La Grange, Illinois, and closely resembles its Swedish prototypes, but with a tougher body shell to comply with American safety requirements. Brian Hollingsworth notes that the AEM-7's 17 percent weight increase over its European counterparts was possible because American lines are built to accommodate significantly greater axle loads.

The AEM-7 is noticeably more powerful than Swedish Rc types so that it can reach higher speeds. The AEM-7 delivers 53,300 pounds tractive effort and up to 7,000 horsepower. Amtrak initially ordered 47 AEM-7s that were delivered in the early 1980s, allowing Amtrak to retire the last of its GG1 fleet in 1981 and reassign the PRR-era *Metroliner* MUs to other duties. Amtrak ordered additional AEM-7s to replace locomotives damaged in accidents.

Commuter agencies established to relieve Conrail (or its predecessors) of its suburban passenger operations have also ordered AEM-7s and derivatives for passenger services. Philadelphia-based South Eastern Pennsylvania Transportation Authority (SEPTA) bought seven AEM-7s and one ALP-44 for push-pull service. Maryland Rail Commuter Service (MARC) has four AEM-7s for its

Pennsylvania's lone SEPTA ALP-44, No. 2308, leads an afternoon passenger train at Bryn Mawr, Pennsylvania, at 6:05 P.M. on April 30, 2003. The ALP-44 is closely related to the Swedish Rc6, though there are a variety of relatively minor external differences, including the porthole windows and headlights, and the cab profile. The Swedish electrics draw power from catenary energized at 15,000 volts at 16.6Hz, while SEPTA's electrics work from 12,000 volts at 60Hz. *Patrick Yough*

The AEM-7 uses a single arm "Favley" pantograph to collect electricity from overhead catenary. *Brian Solomon*

Penn Line Perryville/Baltimore-to-Washington services on the Northeast Corridor. In 1990, NJ Transit, which operates suburban services on several ex-PRR and Delaware, Lackawanna & Western electrified lines in New Jersey, ordered another Rc variation, the ALP-44, built by ASEA's successors, ABB and Adtranz. The ALP-44 is based on the

NJ Transit's ALP-44s are derived from the more advanced Swedish Rc6 and were built by ABB and its successor, Adtranz. NJ Transit uses its ALP-44s in push-pull service on suburban passenger trains. On October 28, 1991, No. 4402 shoves its train toward New York City after making a station stop at Princeton Junction, New Jersey. This locomotive delivers 51,000 pounds starting tractive effort. *Brian Solomon*

more modern Swedish Rc6. As of this writing there are 32 ALP-44s for service on the Northeast Corridor and on former DL&W suburban lines. The DL&W routes, which were initially electrified at 3,000 volts DC in the 1920s, were upgraded to 25,000 volts AC in the mid-1980s.

In the last few years, Amtrak's AEM-7s have been rebuilt with a modern three-phase AC traction system similar to that used by the *Acela Express* trains. These locomotives are designated AEM-7AC and use four inverters per locomotive, one for each traction motor.

Acela Express Trains

Inspired by the high-speed Shinkansen in Japan (the route of the famous "bullet trains" that opened in 1964), the federal government in 1965 funded development of high-speed railway technology in the Northeast Corridor. As a result, moderately high-speed service was introduced in the late 1960s, with electrically powered *Metroliners* (and gas-powered turbo trains on the New York–Boston section) that reached a top speed of 120 miles per hour between New York and Washington, D.C.

Amtrak HHL No. 661 glides across the drawbridge over the Housatonic at South Norwalk in November 2002. These powerful locomotives use the same technology as the *Acela Express* train sets, and feature a similar streamlining treatment. Unlike *Acela Express* power cars, however, they are true locomotives. Since they are more powerful than the older AEM-7s, Amtrak usually assigns the HHLs to long consists. *Brian Solomon*

During the early 1990s, Amtrak took renewed interest in high-speed trains. It imported an X2000 train set from Sweden and an ICE-1 set from Germany for testing on the Northeast Corridor, and for nationwide tours to generate interest in the prospect of high-speed rail.

One hurdle for Amtrak's operations was the end of electric wires at New Haven. Eventually, Congress appropriated funds to complete the electrification to Boston first planned by the New Haven Railroad before World War I. Unlike the traditional systems used on the other part of the Northeast Corridor, the New Haven–to-Boston segment uses a very modern configuration energized

at 25,000 volts (25kV) and 60 cycles. With the completion of electrification, Amtrak introduced a new service, the *Acela Express.*

December 11, 2000, saw the first revenue run of an *Acela Express* between Washington and Boston. Americans were finally able to enjoy high-speed train service. The train is very European in its design. Its interior, as the result of extensive studies, is comfortable, convenient, and a pleasure to ride, though the train still is experiencing mechanical problems.

Acela Express trains were built by a consortium of Bombardier and Alstom and assembled at Barre, Vermont, with some final work performed in New York State. Initially, just one *Acela Express* train was put into service, offering one high-speed roundtrip daily. Eventually more high-speed trains were put into service, offering greater frequency. This service has since been augmented with more conventional trains running on slower schedules.

The *Acela Express* blends French-designed propulsion technology from the state-of-the-art, high-speed Trains à Grande Vitesse (TGV), with a tilting mechanism developed for Canadian Light Rapid Comfortable (LRC) trains in the 1980s. The locomotives do not tilt, only the passenger cars do, as tilting is only necessary for greater passenger comfort at higher speeds and does not actually allow the train to travel faster.

One locomotive, or *power car*, is located at each end of the train set and uses a state-of-the-art, three-phase propulsion system, similar to that employed on other high-speed trains around the world. The first modern three-phase AC traction was commercially employed on the German Class 120 electric locomotives designed in the late 1970s. By the late 1980s, AC traction was in use in Germany, Japan, and France for high-speed services. Three-phase alternating current traction enables the train to accelerate to high speeds very quickly and requires fewer electric motors to accomplish the same job as conventional direct current technology. AC traction motors are more powerful, weigh less, and require far less maintenance than conventional DC traction motors.

Modern AC traction has been made possible by advances in semiconductor technology and microprocessor computer controls. Early three-phase electrics—such as the Great Northern's and those that used phase splitters, such as those built for the Virginian and Norfolk & Western in the 1920s—were designed to use synchronous motors

Amtrak HHLs Nos. 660 and 662 whisk train No.197 along the Northeast Corridor at Jersey Avenue, New Jersey, at 5:44 P.M. on September 22, 2001. In the distance on the adjacent track is a set of NJ Transit's *Arrow III* multiple-units. *Patrick Yough.*

An *Acela Express* train blasts through the new station at Old Saybrook, Connecticut, in October 2002. Although billed as a high-speed train, the *Acela Express* is, in effect, primarily a service improvement. *Brian Solomon*

operating at a constant speed. These early locomotives worked well hauling heavy tonnage over mountain grades, but their motors' limitations did not lend to general applications. Modern three-phase AC propulsion regulates motor speed by modulating current frequency with sophisticated electronic thyristor controls called *gate turnoff* circuits or *GTOs*. This same technology is also employed on some modern diesel-electric locomotives used in heavy freight services around the country, such as EMD's SD70MAC and GE's AC4400CW.

The *Acela Express* locomotives are multivoltage and can draw power from the various voltages now used to energize different sections of the Northeast Corridor: 11,000 volts (11kV) at 25Hz, 13,200 volts (13.2kV) at 60Hz (nominal), and 25,000 volts (25kV) at 60Hz. The voltages are a function of the complex electrical history the different sections of the Northeast Corridor and remain to accommodate older existing suburban trains operating over the individual segments.

Each *Acela Express* power car carries a main transformer that is silicone oil–cooled, and a

Among the newest electrics operating in the United States are NJ Transit's ALP-46s, based on the German class 101 introduced in 1996 and built by ADtranz. Using a standard B-B wheel arrangement, they produce 7,108 horsepower, weigh 198,400 pounds, and deliver 71,000 pounds starting tractive effort. They are designed to draw power from three different standard overhead systems and use modern GTO electronics to control three-phase AC traction motors which give the locomotive significantly more starting power than old DC traction types. Here, NJ transit No. 4607 zips through Linden, New Jersey on June 6, 2003. *Patrick Yough*

rectifier cooled with liquid glycol. Single-phase AC from the catenary passes through the transformer and rectifier, which uses GTO circuits to produce 2,750 volts DC. The DC power is then filtered and sent through inverters for conversion to three-phase AC using banks of GTO circuits. The locomotive uses a pair of inverters to drive traction motors, and a third inverter for head-end power requirements. Head-end power is used to provide onboard electricity for heating and lighting. Inverters enable the frequency regulation necessary to control the speed of the traction motors. Two traction inverters each drive two rugged 4-FXA-4559C three-phase, four-pole, asynchronous AC traction motors per power car. The motors use a squirrel-cage induction design and engage axles using a 71:23 gear ratio. Drive wheels are 40 inches in diameter, also typical of modern diesel-electric locomotives. Weight on the driving wheels is a maximum of 200,000 pounds.

In conjunction with the Northeast Corridor electrification extension to Boston, Amtrak had many of its AEM-7s rebuilt with modern three-phase AC traction propulsion. These locomotives now carry the AEM-7AC designation and are easily identified by the additional electrical equipment on their roofs. Amtrak No. 944 leads train No. 19, *Crescent,* at Norwood, Pennsylvania, on May 3, 2003. Traditionally this train was too heavy for a single AEM-7 and often warranted an E60C. *Patrick Yough*

An AEM-7AC rolling eastward with a three-car train along Long Island Sound near Niantic, Connecticut, catches the glint of the setting sun. East of New Haven, the wires are energized at 25,000 volts at 60Hz. *Brian Solomon*

Each locomotive can provide up to 6,169 continuous horsepower, giving the train a total of 12,338 horsepower. The power cars are 69 feet, 7 inches long. High horsepower is needed for rapid acceleration and to maintain continuous high speeds. Maximum designed speed is 165 miles per hour, although maximum speed in regular service is limited to 150 miles per hour, which makes it the fastest in North America by a long margin.

An *Acela Express* train starting from a station emits a high-pitched *Schwizzzzzft* as it speeds away from the platform. These are the sounds of the high-voltage electronics that transform, rectify, and control the current used for traction and train electricity. It is a very different array of sounds than those produced by an old side-rod electric or a classic 1930s GG1.

BIBLIOGRAPHY

Books

Alymer-Small, Sidney. *The Art of Railroading, Vol. VIII.* Chicago, 1908.

American Railroad Journal, 1966. San Marino, Calif., 1965.

Armstrong, John H. *The Railroad: What It Is, What It Does.* Omaha, Nebr., 1982.

Bean, W. L. *Twenty Years of Electrical Operation on the New York, New Haven and Hartford Railroad.* East Pittsburgh, Pa., 1927.

Bezilla, Michael. *Electric Traction on the Pennsylvania Railroad 1895–1968.* State College, Pa., 1981.

Burch, Edward P. *Electric Traction for Railway Trains.* New York, 1911.

Bush, Donald, J. *The Streamlined Decade.* New York, 1975.

Condit, Carl. *Port of New York, Vol. 1 & 2.* Chicago, 1980, 1981.

Dover, A. T. *Electric Traction.* London, 1925.

Droege, John A. *Freight Terminals and Trains.* New York, 1912.

———. *Passenger Terminals and Trains.* New York, 1916.

Garmany, John B. *Southern Pacific Dieselization.* Edmonds, Wash., 1985.

Harris, Ken. *World Electric Locomotives.* London, 1981.

Haut, F. J. G. *The History of the Electric Locomotive.* London, 1969.

———. *The Pictorial History of Electric Locomotives.* Cranbury, N.J., 1970.

Herrick, Albert, B. *Practical Electric Railway Hand Book.* New York, 1906.

Hinde, D. W. and M. Hinde. *Electric and Diesel-Electric Locomotives.* London, 1948.

Hollingsworth, Brian. *Modern Trains.* London, 1985.

Hollingsworth, Brian and Arthur Cook. *Modern Locomotives.* London, 1983.

Marks, Lionel S. *Mechanical Engineers' Handbook, 3rd Ed.* New York, 1930.

Marre, Louis, A. *Diesel Locomotives: The First 50 Years.* Waukesha, Wisc., 1995.

Marre, Louis A. and Jerry A. Pinkepank. *The Contemporary Diesel Spotter's Guide.* Milwaukee, Wisc., 1985.

Marre, Louis A. and Paul K. Withers. *The Contemporary Diesel Spotter's Guide, 2000 Ed.* Halifax, Pa., 2000.

Middleton, William D. *North Shore . . . America's Fastest Interturban.* San Marino, Calif., 1963.

———. *South Shore . . . The Last Interturban.* San Marino, Calif., 1970.

———. *When the Steam Railroads Electrified.* Milwaukee, Wisc., 1974.

———. *Grand Central . . . The World's Greatest Railway Terminal.* San Marino, Calif., 1977.

———. *From Bullets to BART.* Chicago, 1989.

———. *Manhattan Gateway: New York's Pennsylvania Station.* Waukesha, Wisc., 1996.

Pinkepank, Jerry A. *The Second Diesel Spotter's Guide.* Milwaukee, 1973.

Ransome-Wallis, P. *World Railway Locomotives*. New York, 1959.

Reagan, H. C., Jr. *Locomotive Mechanism and Engineering*. New York, 1894.

Reckenzaun, Anthony. *Electric Traction on Railways and Tramways*. London, 1892.

Reid, H. *The Virginian Railway*. Milwuakee, Wisc., 1961.

Solomon, Brian. *The American Diesel Locomotive*. Osceola, Wisc., 2000.

———. *Super Steam Locomotives*. Osceola, Wisc., 2000.

———. *Locomotive*. St. Paul, Minn., 2001.

Staufer, Alvin F. *Pennsy Power III*. Medina, Ohio, 1968.

Staufer, Alvin F. and Edward L. May. *New York Central's Later Power 1910–1968*. Medina, Ohio, 1981.

Stevens, John R. *Pioneers of Electric Railroading*. New York, 1991.

Trewman, H. F. *Electrifcation of Railways*. London, 1920.

Winchester, Clarence. *Railway Wonders of the World, Vol. 1 & 2*. London, 1935.

Zimmerman, Karl R. *The Remarkable GG1*. New York, 1905.

Periodicals

Baldwin Locomotives. Philadelphia, Pa. [no longer published]

CTC Board. Ferndale, Wash.

Diesel Era. Halifax, Pa.

Diesel Railway Traction (supplement to *Railway Gazette*). U.K. [merged into *Railway Gazette*]

Jane's World Railways. London.

Modern Railways. Surrey, U.K.

Official Guide to the Railways. New York.

Pacific RailNews. Waukesha, Wisc. [no longer published]

Passenger Train Journal. Waukesha, Wisc. [no longer published]

Railroad History (formerly *Railway and Locomotive Historical Society Bulletin*). Boston, Mass.

Railway Age. Chicago and New York.

The Railway Gazette. London.

Today's Railways. Sheffield, U.K.

TRAINS. Waukesha, Wisc.

Vintage Rails. Waukesha, Wisc. [no longer published]

INDEX

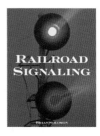

Railroad Signaling
ISBN 0-7603-1360-1

Modern Locomotives
ISBN 0-7603-1258-3

GE Locomotives
ISBN 0-7603-1361-X

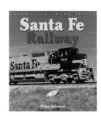

Santa Fe Railway
ISBN 0-7603-1358-08

New Haven Railroad
ISBN 0-7603-1441-1

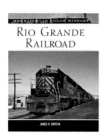

Rio Grande Railroad
ISBN 0-7603-1442-X

20th Century Limited
ISBN 0-7603-1422-5

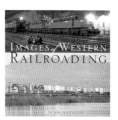

**Images of Western
Railroading**
ISBN 0-7603-1574-4

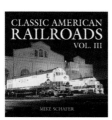

**Classic American
Railroads, Vol. III**
ISBN 0-7603-1649-X